Well Seasoned
Savoring Life's Lessons

Rebecca webb Wilson

Inspire on Purpose Publishing
Irving, Texas

Well Seasoned: Savoring Life's Lessons

Inspire On Purpose Publishing
(888) 403-2727
http://inspireonpurpose.com
The Platform Publisher™

Printed in the United States of America

Library of Congress Control Number: 2014913221

ISBN 10: 0-9898008-6-5
ISBN 13: 978-0-9898008-6-0

To my amazing husband Spence, with whom I have traveled through most of my seasons. The years just get better. Thank you for helping me picture life in a variety of new and wonderful ways. It's never boring.

CONTENTS

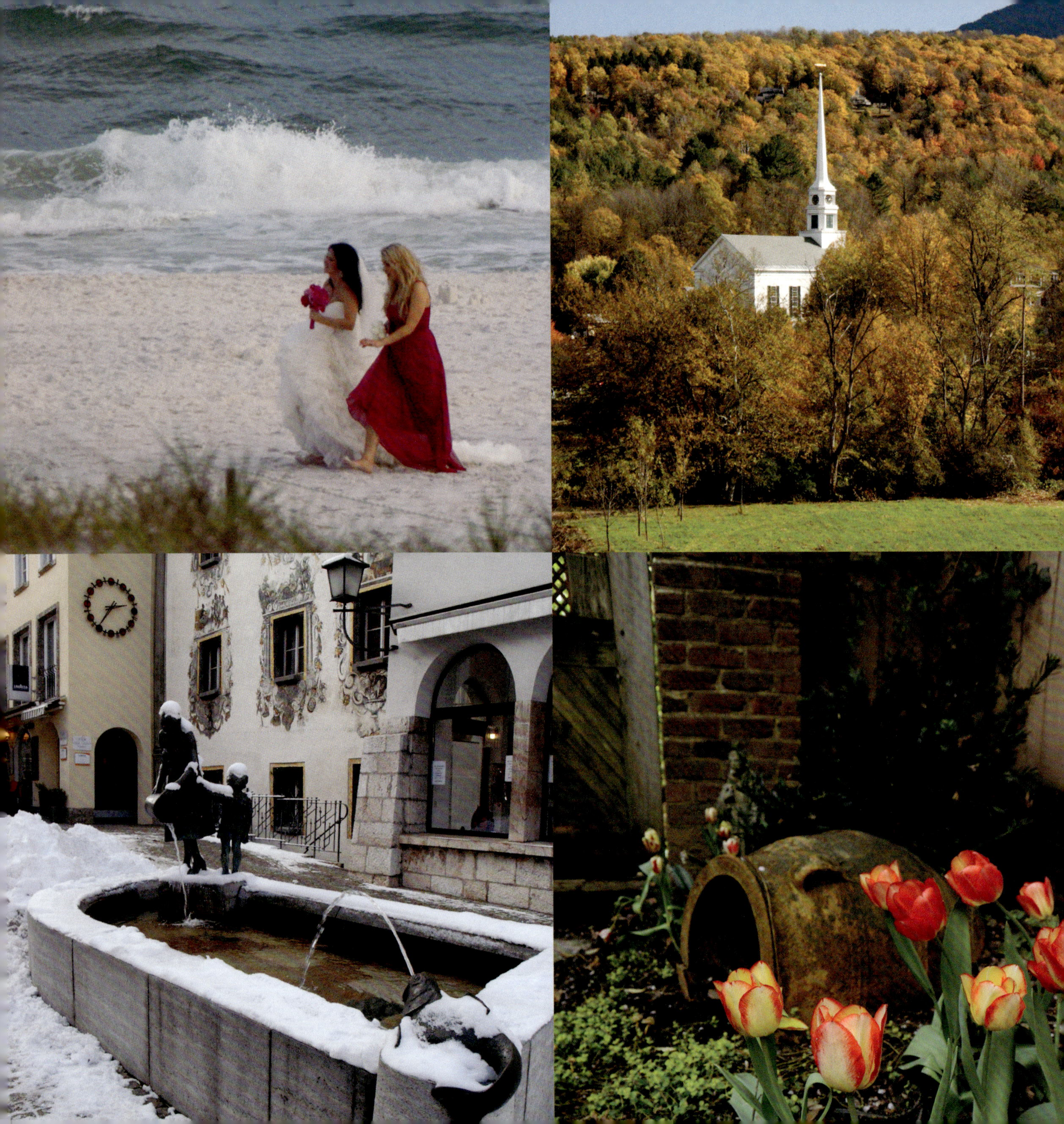

Introduction

For several years, a couple of days a week, I have gone for a run early in the morning. I'm not naturally a morning person, but the discipline has been good for me, and I know the exercise helps me stay fit physically and mentally. One morning, I began thinking how radically the roles of age and gender have changed in the United States from the traditional days of our parents and grandparents.

That so many folks ages fifty and above would routinely run and even compete in races was unheard of fifty years ago. After all, in the late 1950s, the average life expectancy of both genders and all cultures in the U.S. was only 69.7 years.

As a passionate nature photographer, I'd long considered writing a book about the seasons of life. On my run, I realized that I no longer thought winter and the dying of things appropriately represented the latter stage of life, nor did spring always have to be seen as the beginning.

There are several ways to measure how a given set of months constitutes a specific season. Astronomically, the seasons change on the date of the equinoxes (when daylight and darkness receive an equal number of hours) and the solstices (the longest and shortest days of the year).

By that calculation, spring begins on March 21, an equinox. Summer begins on June 21, the summer solstice, which is the longest day of the year. September 21, the other equinox, marks the beginning of autumn. December 22, the shortest day of the year, is the winter solstice.

In the northern hemisphere, meteorologists adopt a convention: winter consists of December, January, and February, not the tidy trio of January, February, and March that our calendars reflect. By extension, spring is comprised of March, April, and May and so forth.

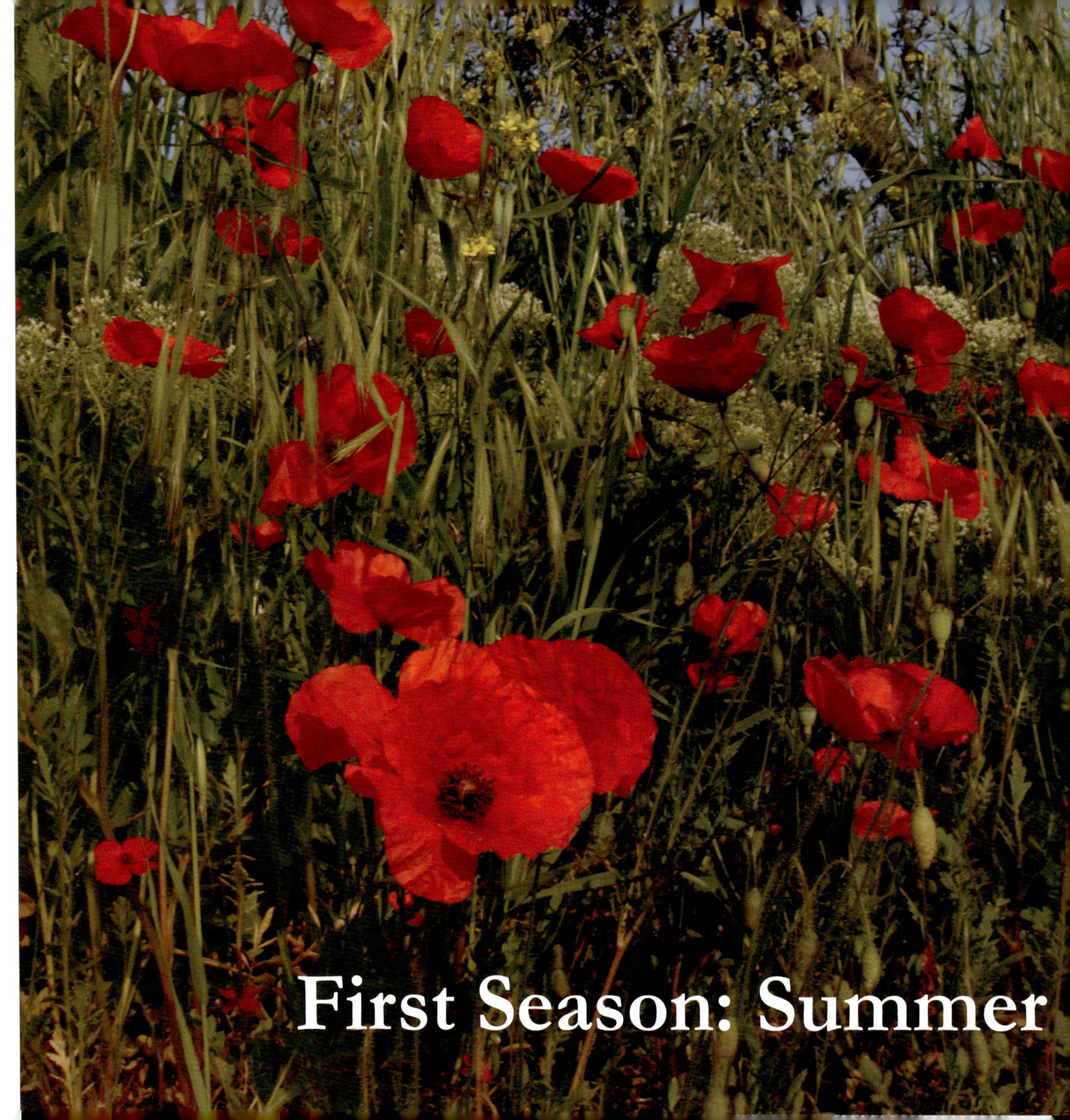

First Season: Summer

While I Am Writing a Poem to Celebrate Summer, the Meadowlark Begins to Sing

by Mary Oliver

Sixty-seven years, oh Lord, to look at the clouds,
the trees in deep, moist summer,

daisies and morning glories
opening every morning

their small, ecstatic faces—
Or maybe I should just say

how I wish I had a voice
like the meadowlark's,

sweet, clear, and reliably
slurring all day long

from the fencepost, or the long grass
where it lives

in a tiny but adequate grass hut
beside the mullein and the everlasting,

the faint-pink roses
that have never been improved, but come to bud

then open like little soft sighs
under the meadowlark's whistle, its breath-praise,

its thrill-song, its anthem, its thanks, its
alleluia. Alleluia, oh Lord.

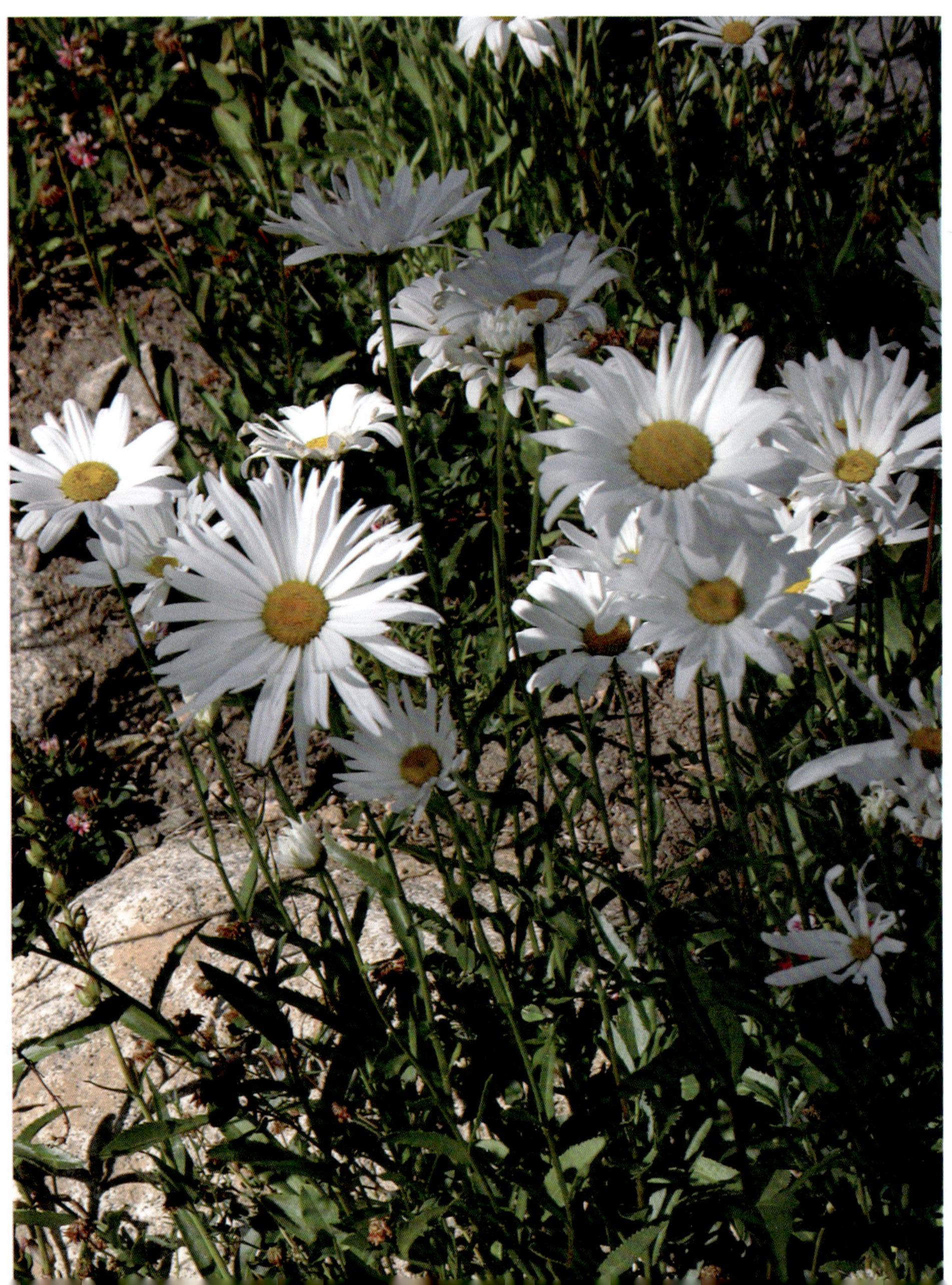

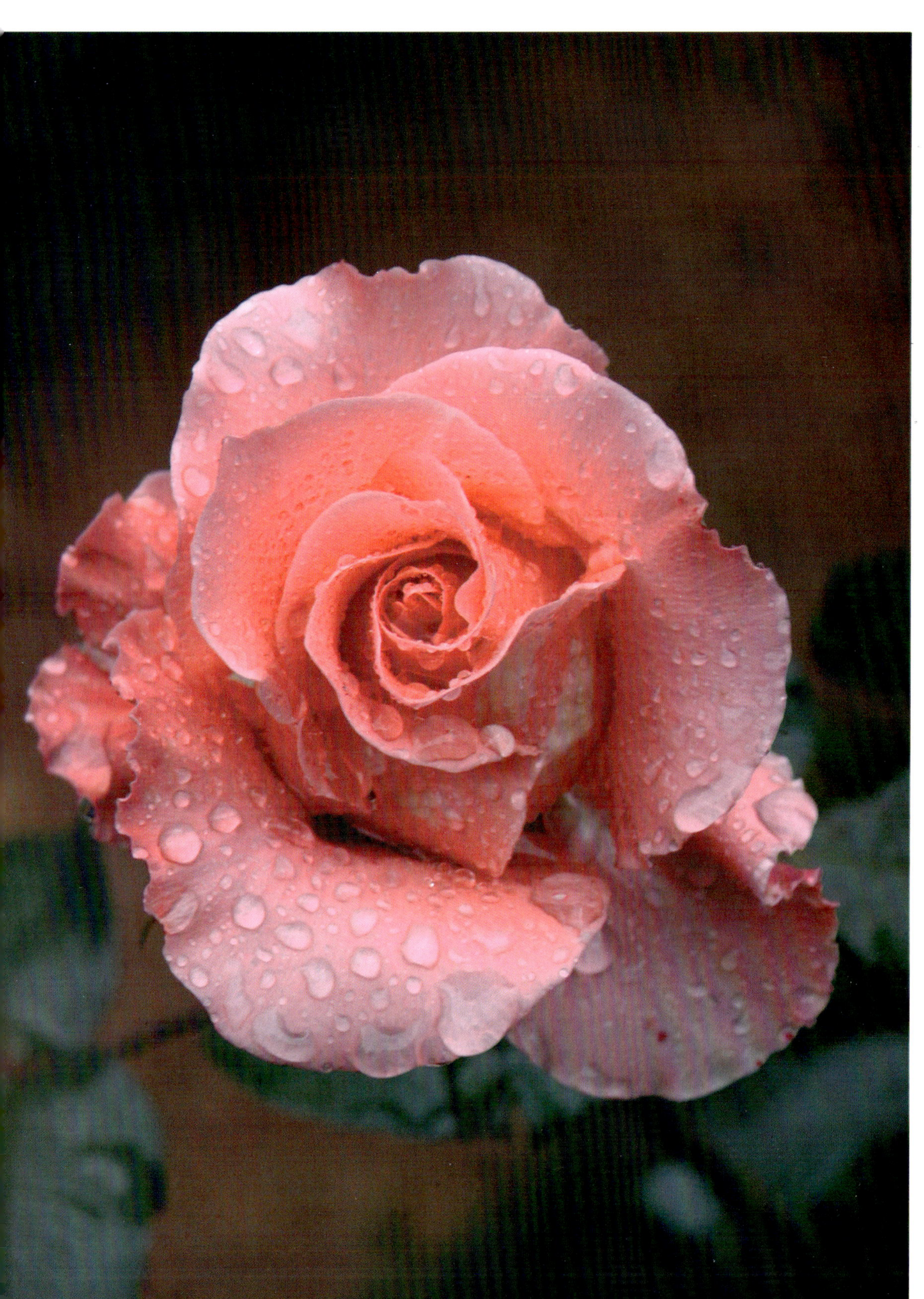

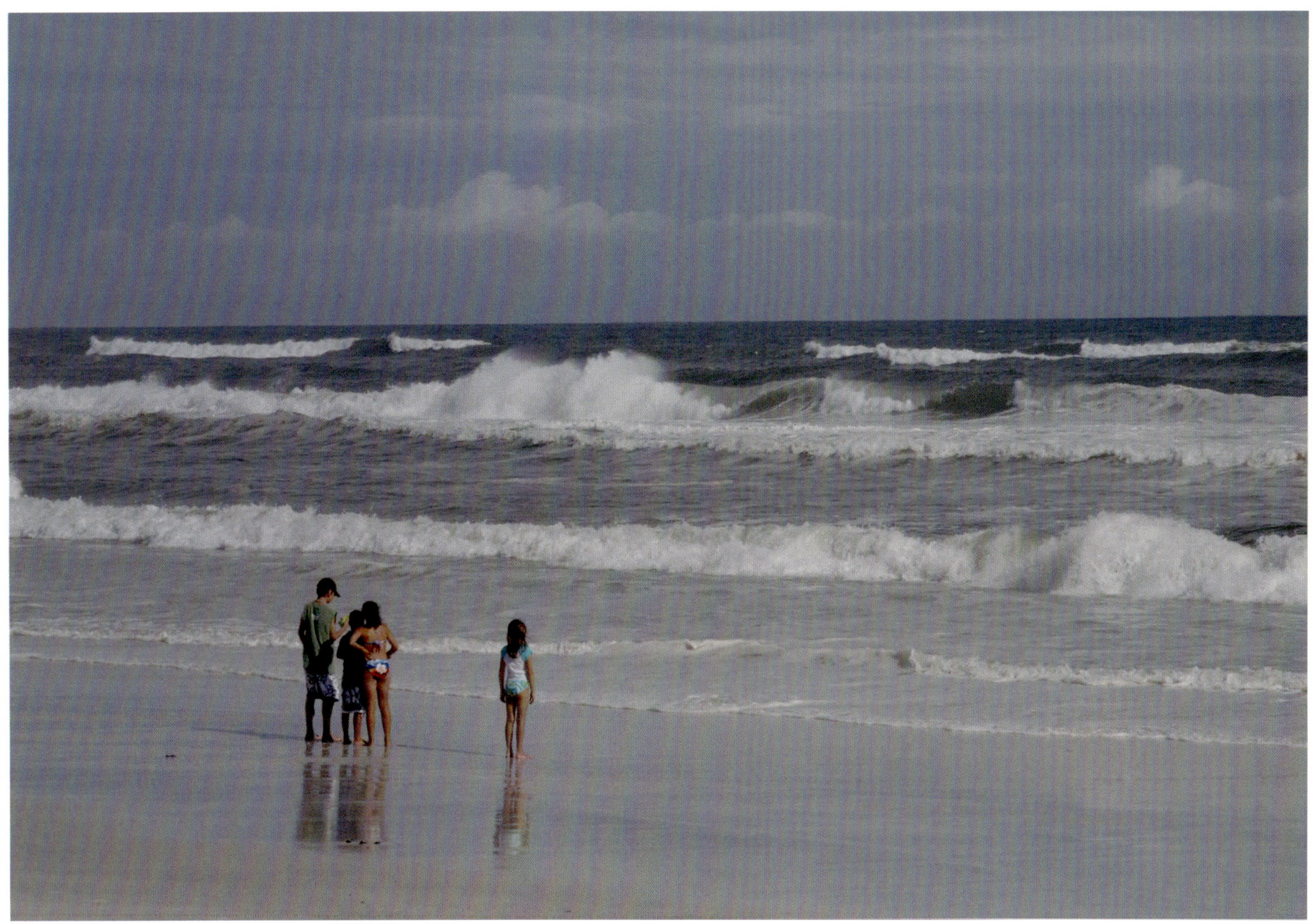

Remember learning to swim? For me, it was a scary time. The little kids had to take lessons early in the morning when we were not quite awake. The freezing cold water certainly woke me but also inhibited my ability to concentrate. I shook throughout the whole class, partly from the chill, partly from my fear of drowning.

Not everyone was so afflicted. A few fish jumped right in and glided off, seemingly as comfortable in this new medium as I was walking on the ground. I did learn to stay afloat,

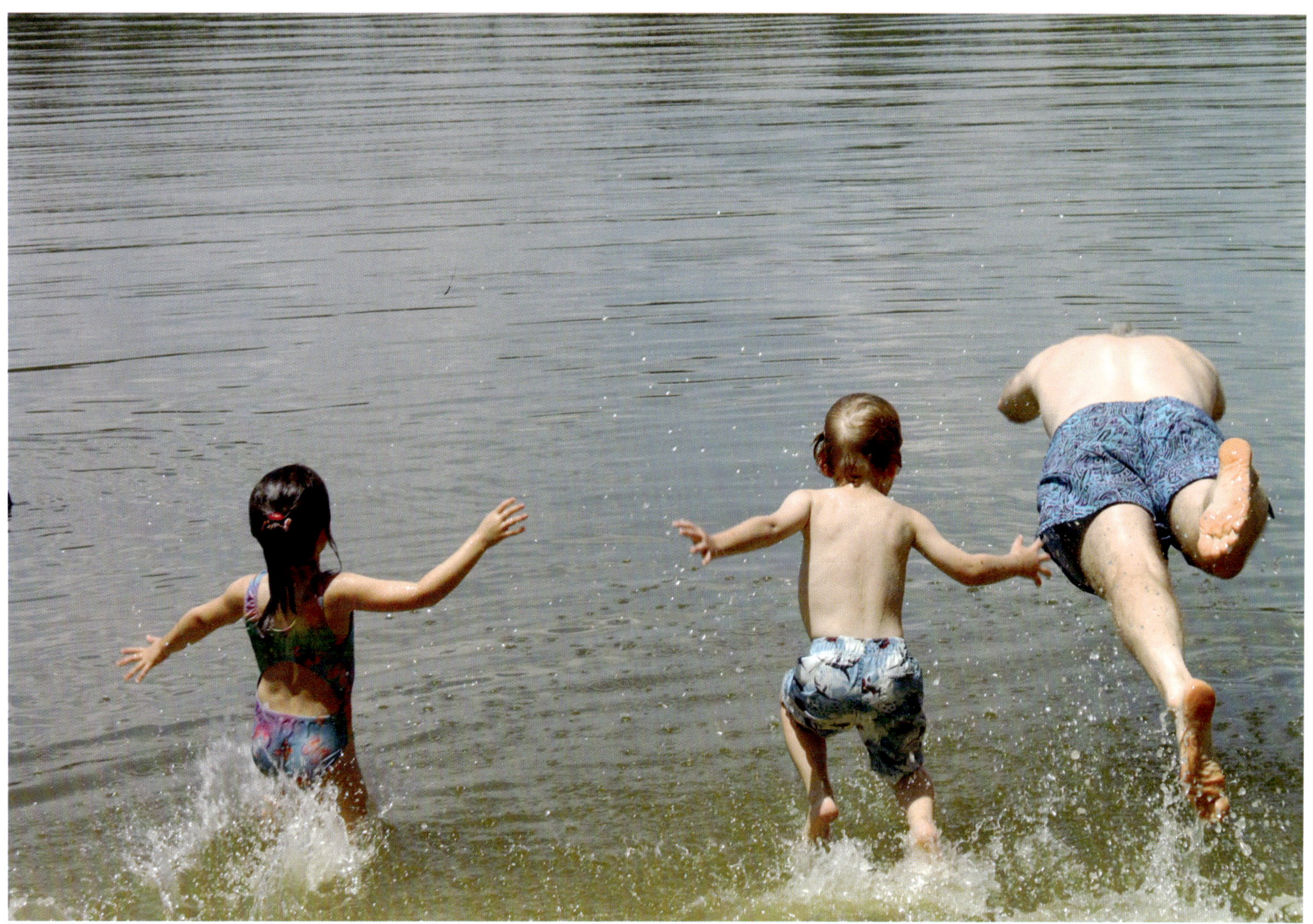

but I lacked grace, style, and endurance. Survival is all I can claim, plus an admiration for those who excelled, which at the time seemed to include virtually everyone else.

Think of the first twenty years on earth as two decades of summer in which we learn to swim through life.

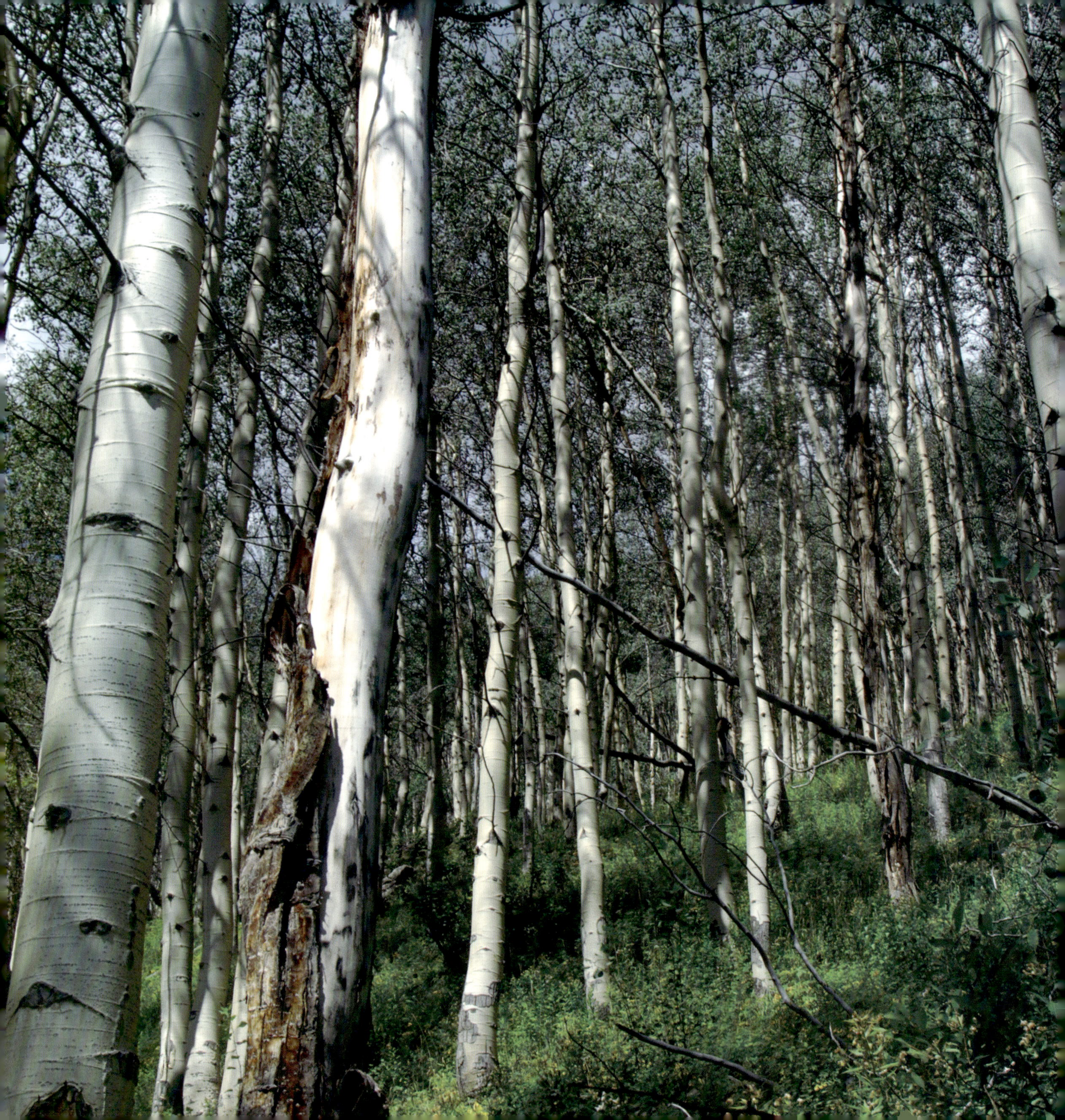

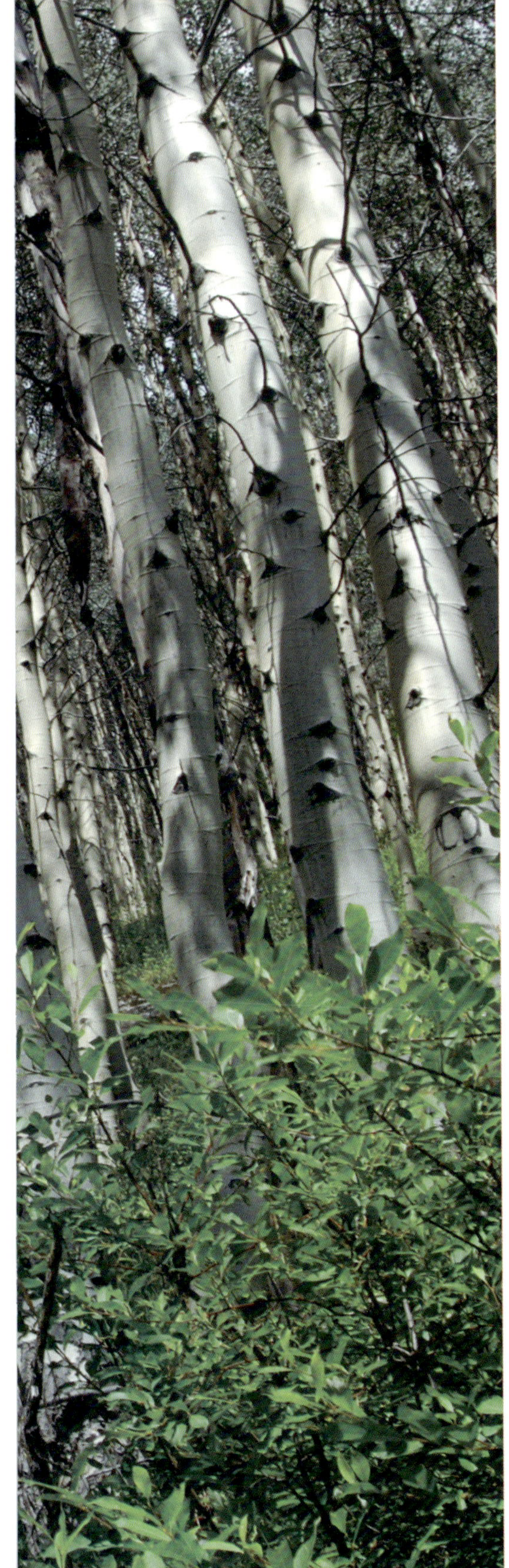

As children and teens, we spent a lot of time playing outside. My generation grew up alongside the beginnings of television, but in those early days, the first TVs (black and white only, with few selections and limited programming) were not common. Television was a novelty, and fortunately for us, it didn't readily supplant the allure of playing "Kick the Can" or "Hide and Seek" until dark, bath, and bedtime.

A vacant lot was a field; a few trees became a jungle or dense forest; a ditch was a dangerous river. A great climbing tree like a mimosa could be the Swiss Family Robinson's massive treetop home, while the bean pods hanging from its limbs went into pretend soup.

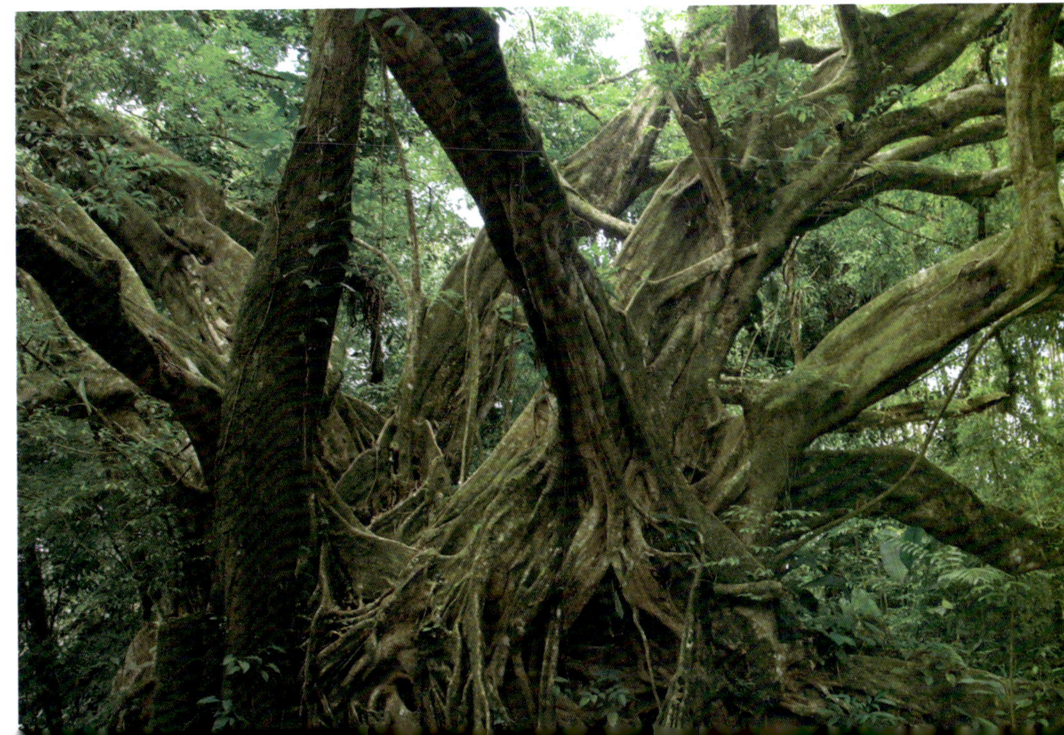

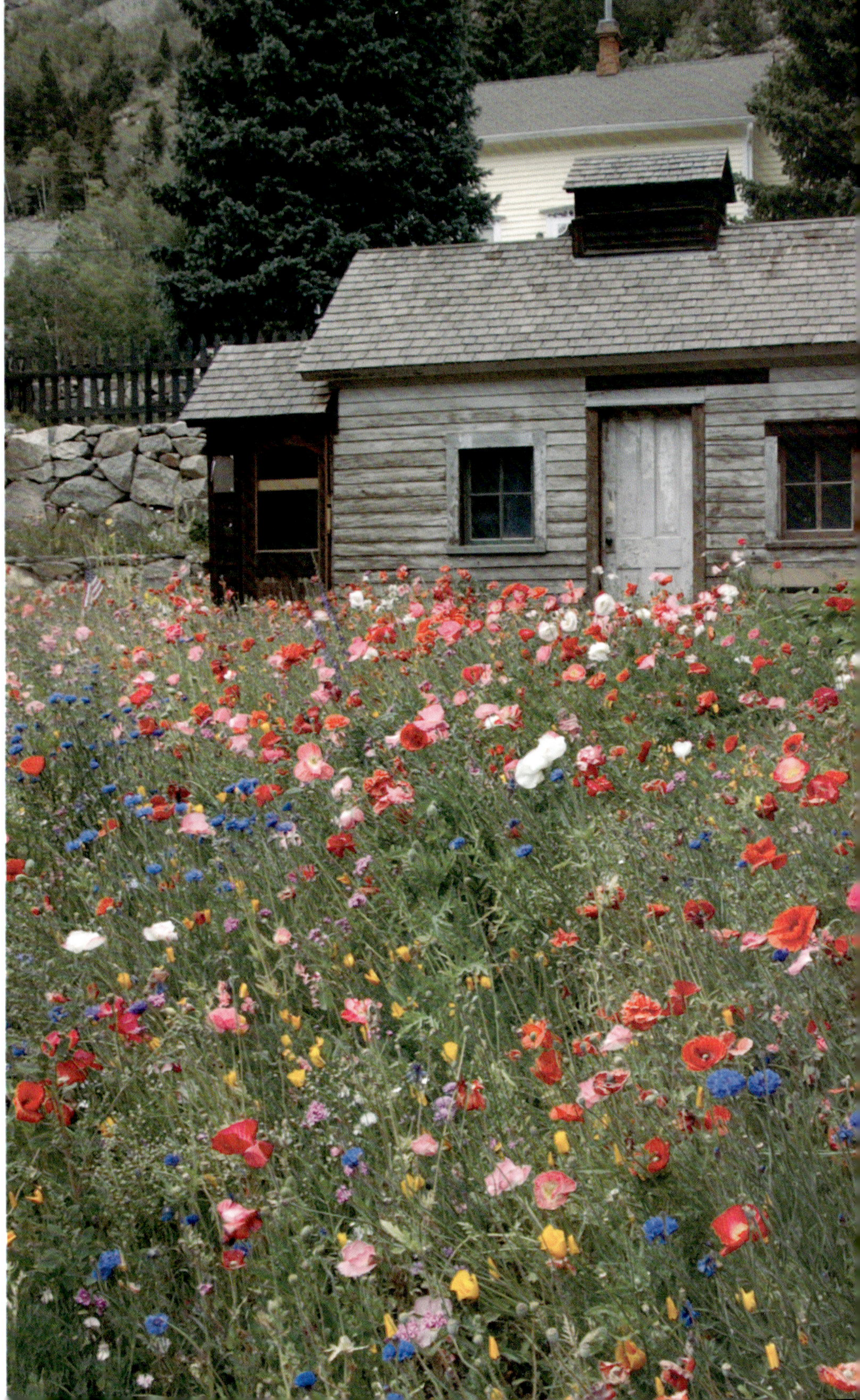

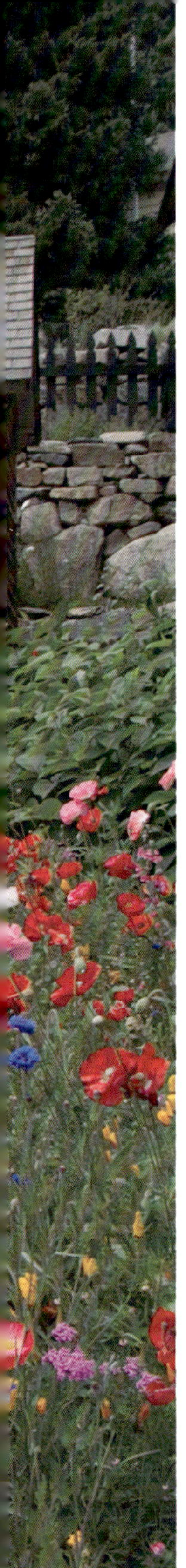

Those early years were times of unending discovery, especially about the natural world.

We saw an abundance of beauty around every corner and an amazing diversity in flowers, birds, and people.

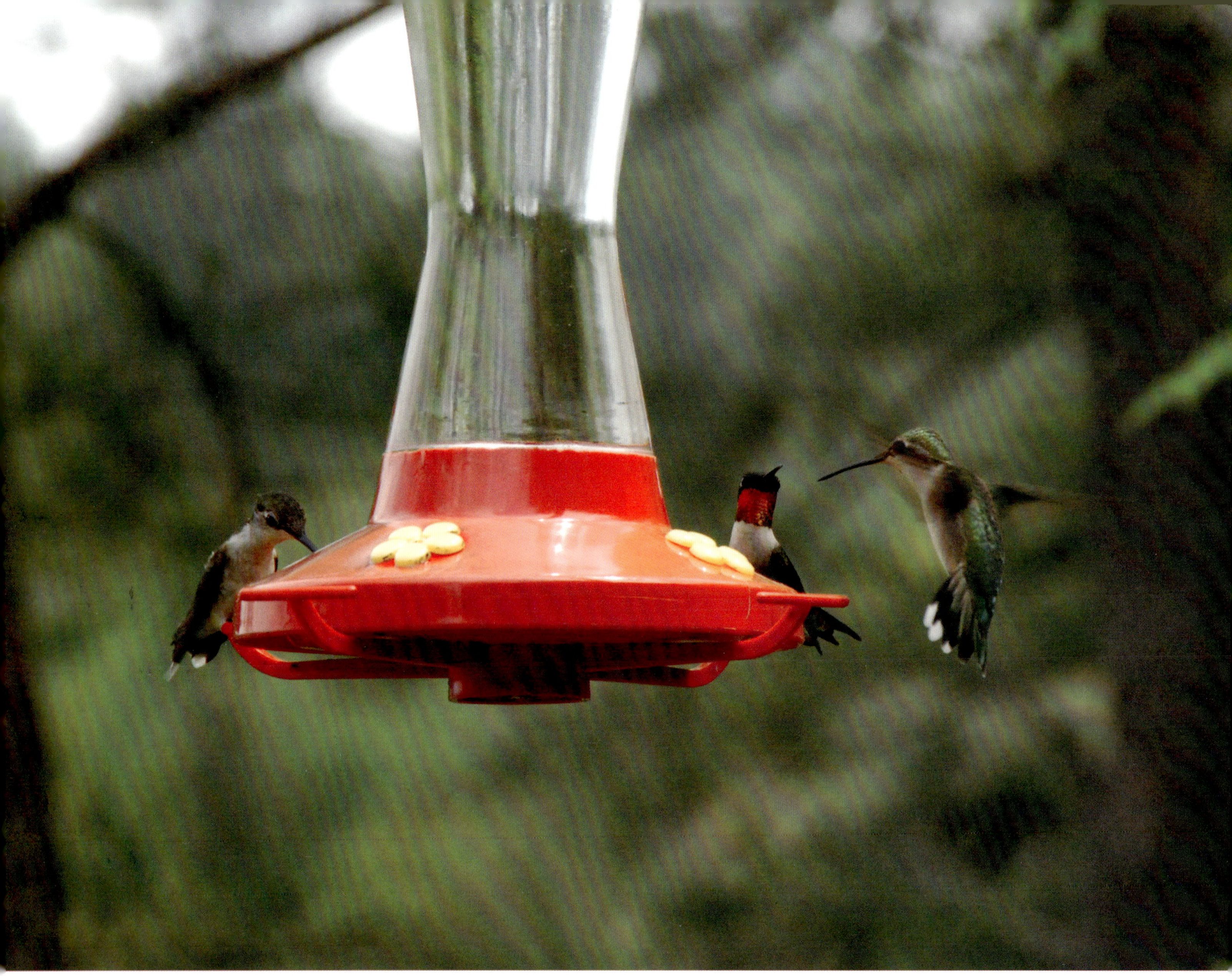

Ah, the wonder of first seeing fireflies, hummingbirds, and butterflies. The taste of mint leaves, the smell of honeysuckle, the sweetness of strawberries picked warm in the sun. All these firsts or something like them awakened our senses and created a curiosity for trying new things.

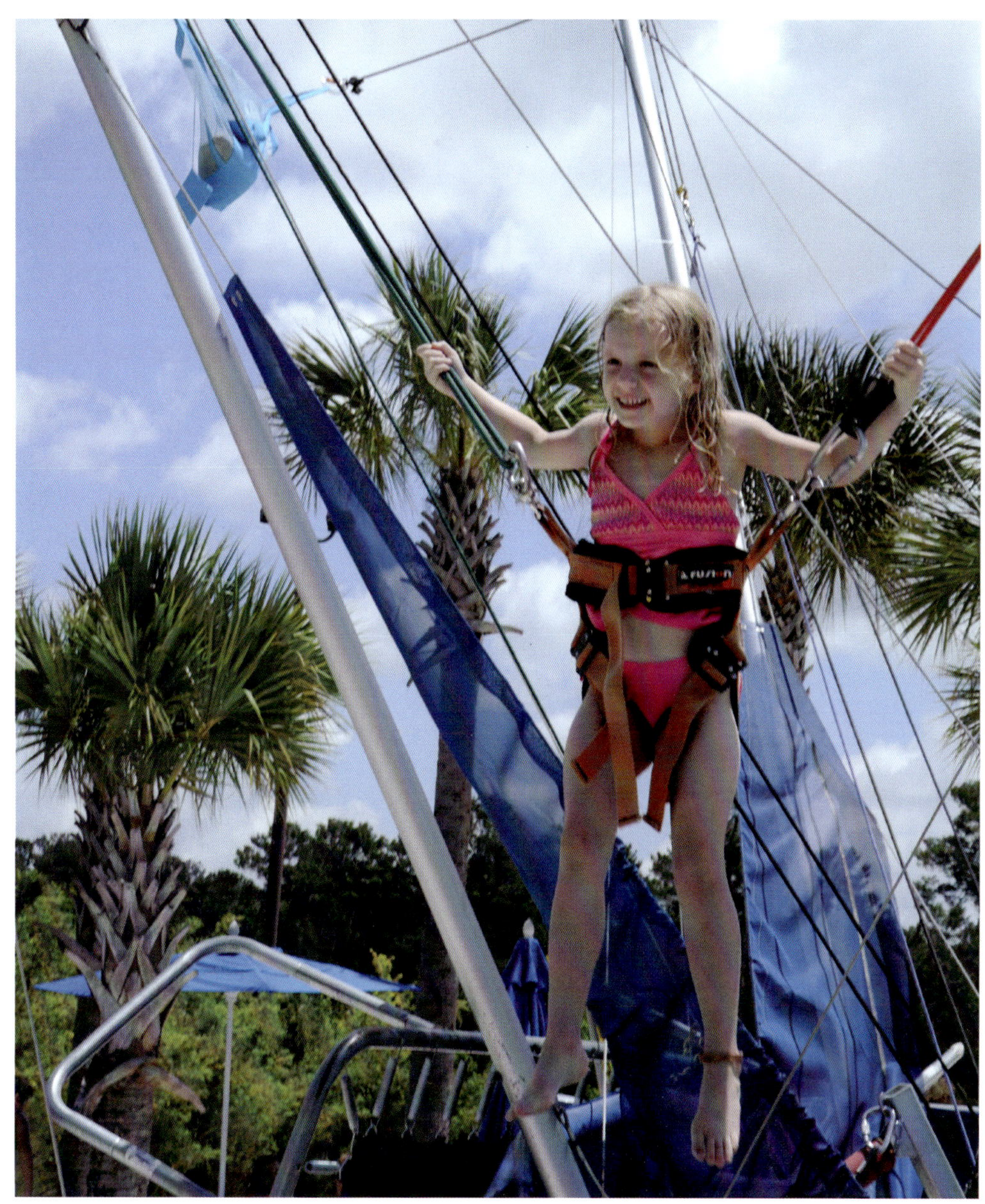

Today, lakes remind us of camping with good friends or church groups and of family trips together. Picnicking, swimming, fishing… All these activities call back those carefree days of summer when we just had to show up. Nothing much else was expected. We experimented with all the options open to us.

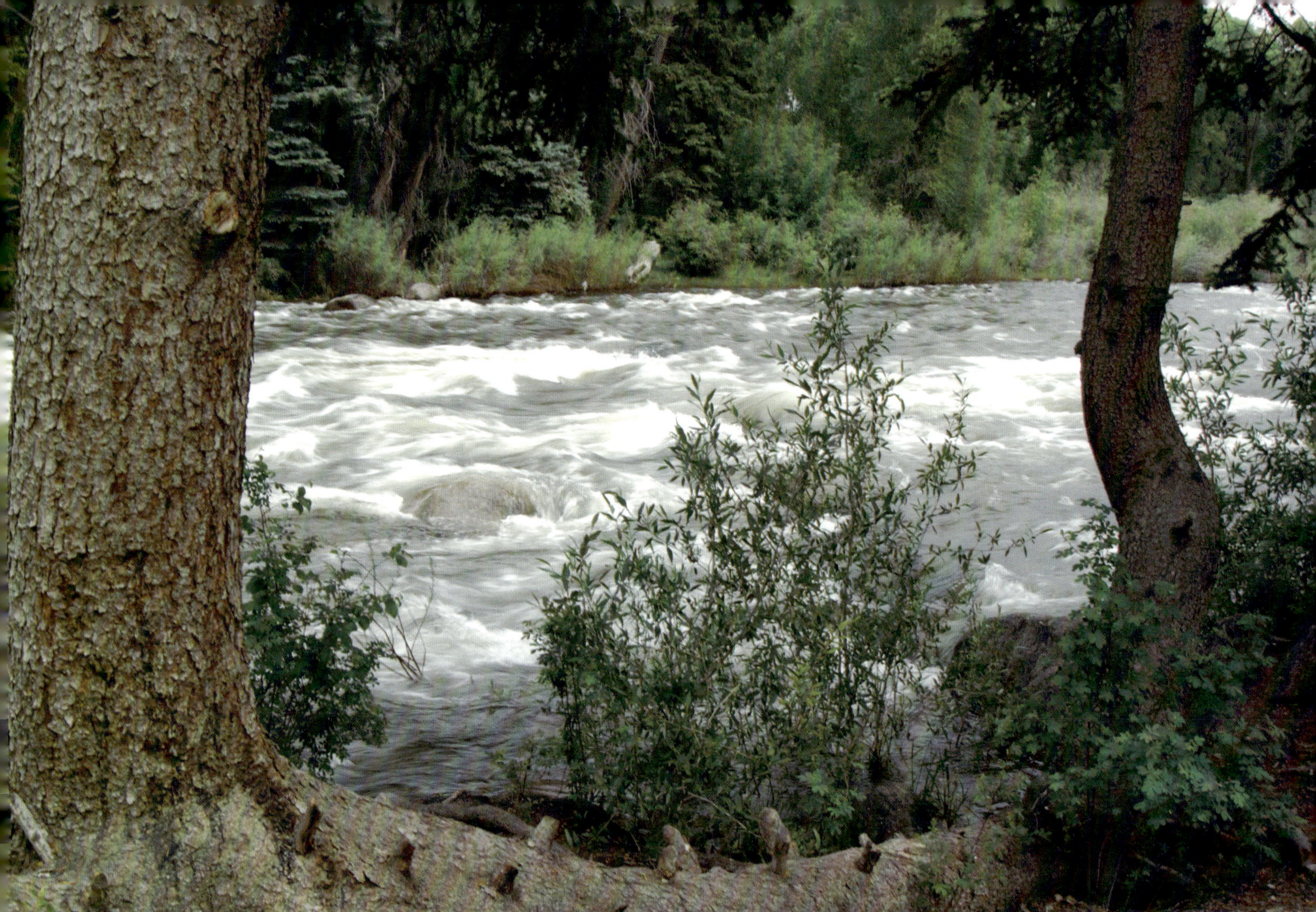

As we stepped out on our individual journeys, we sometimes ran into difficulties. Like rapids in a fast-moving river, we learned how quickly the world could change, but each obstacle helped us adapt and adjust to the challenges.

Often, in retrospect, these were the times we grew the most. Some dogs, we learned, were not as friendly as our own, nor were some people. Cats didn't really need us, nor did all the folks who called us family.

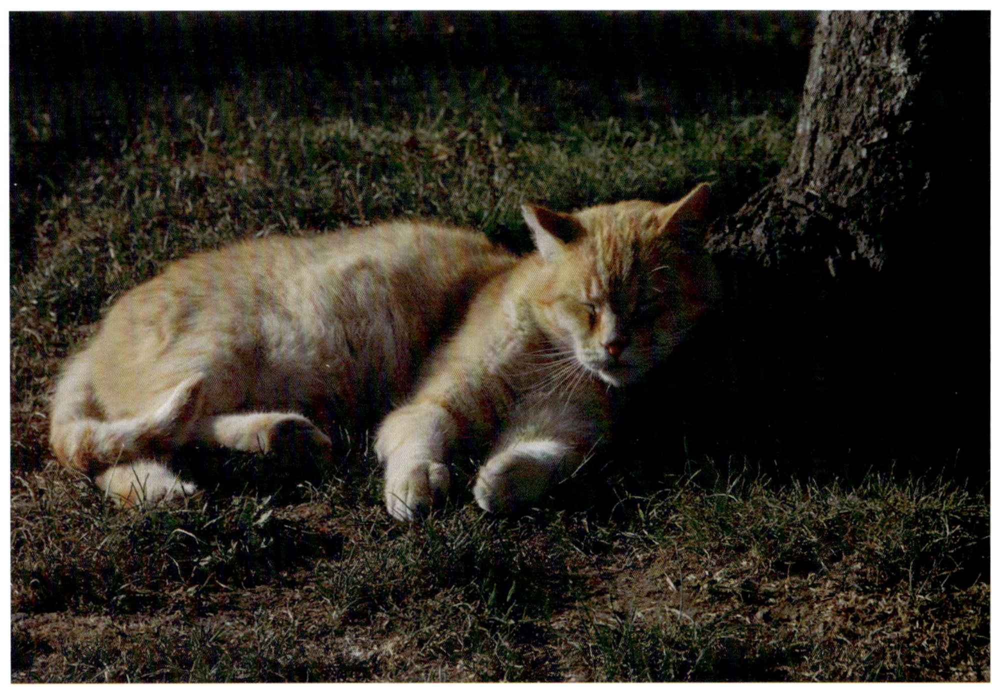

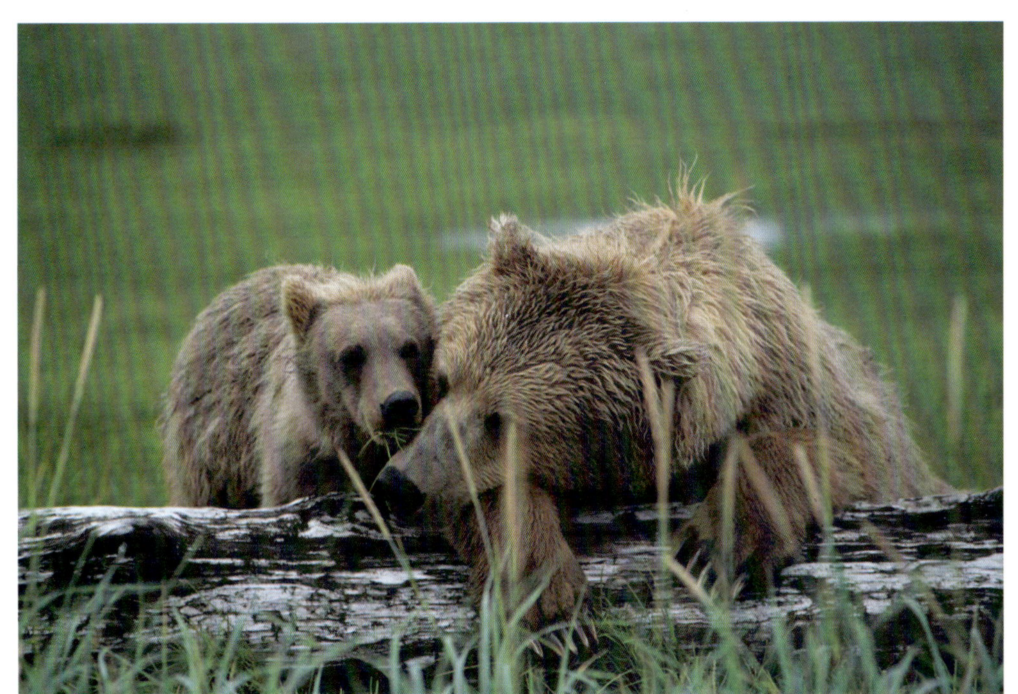

Not everyone grew up in the greatly desired loving home with two parents to support them physically and emotionally. Some tasted fear and confusion from the onset because of neglect or abuse from the very people who brought them into this world. Trust became an issue.

In spite of difficult backgrounds, many found new supports. A Sunday School teacher, a grandparent, a teacher, a guidance counselor: someone who stood there to offer direction and encouragement. These people were bright rainbows in the clouds of life.

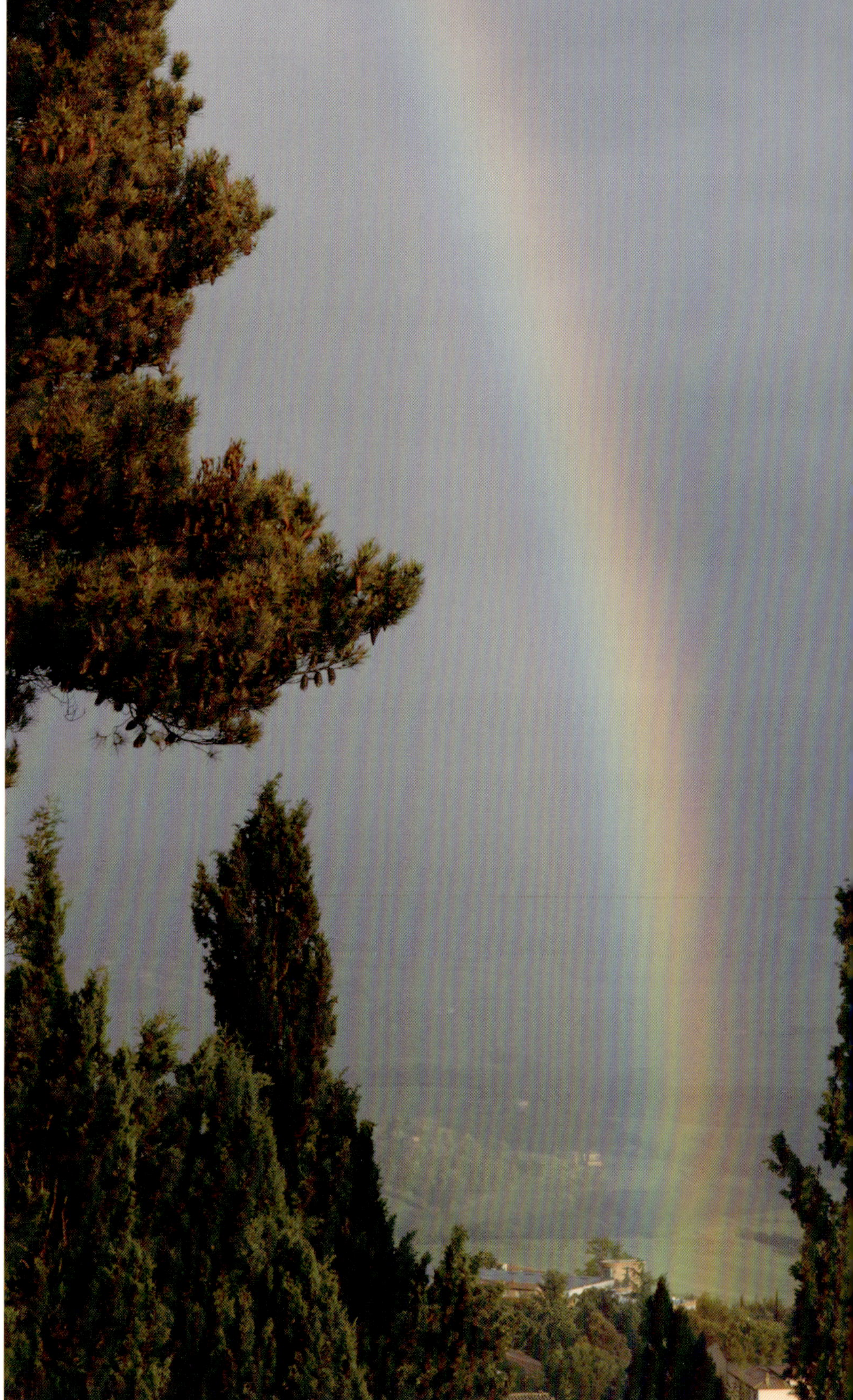

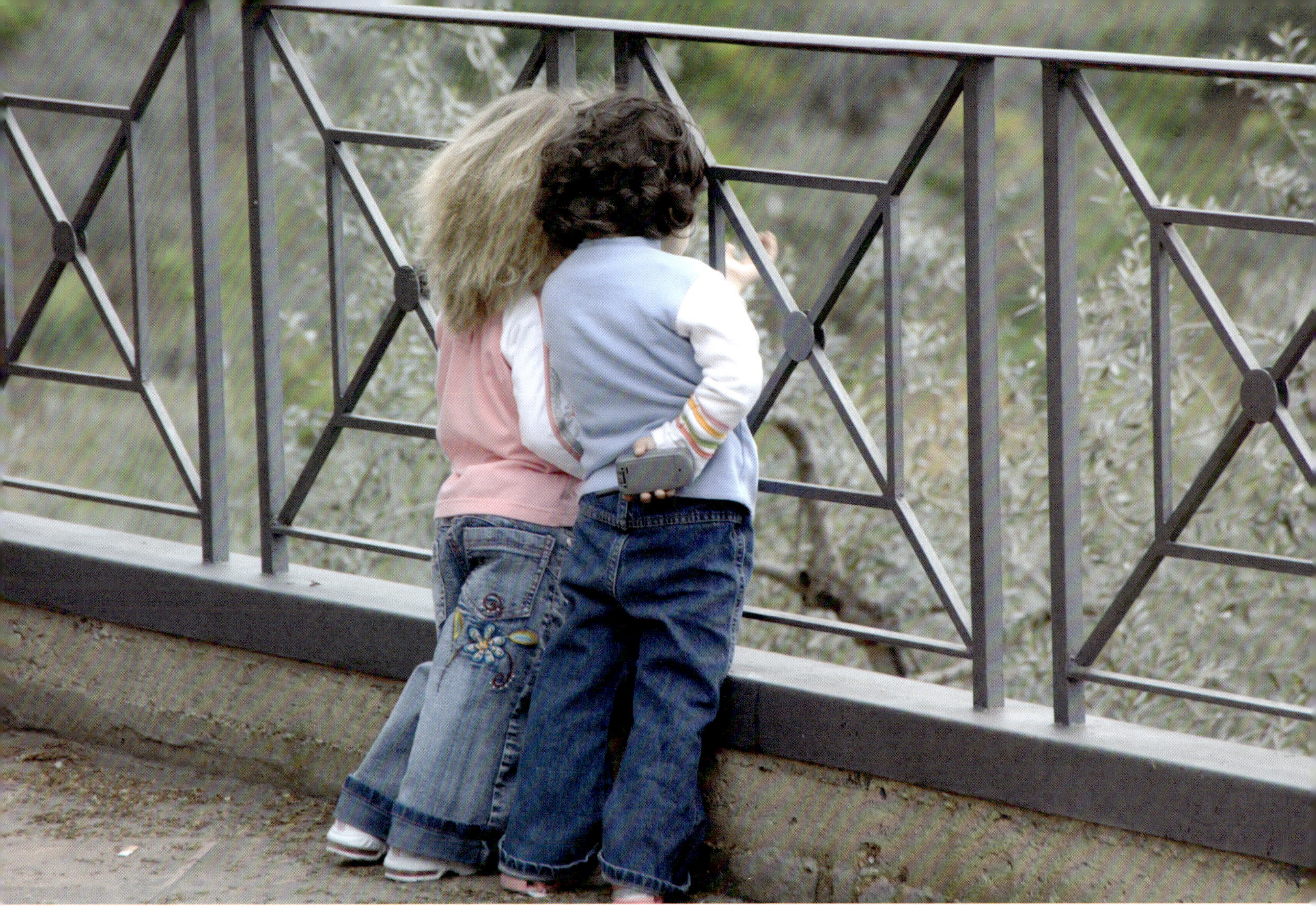

Our best friend in the fourth grade might still be hanging in there in the twelfth, but more likely than not, as we changed schools or cities, another friend moved in and assumed that role.

Then there was that first love affair. Ah, the sweet pain of that awakening, lasting anywhere from days to decades. We eventually learned that we really enjoyed having a special person in our lives, and many of us made concessions in our singleness to become a couple. Some began families.

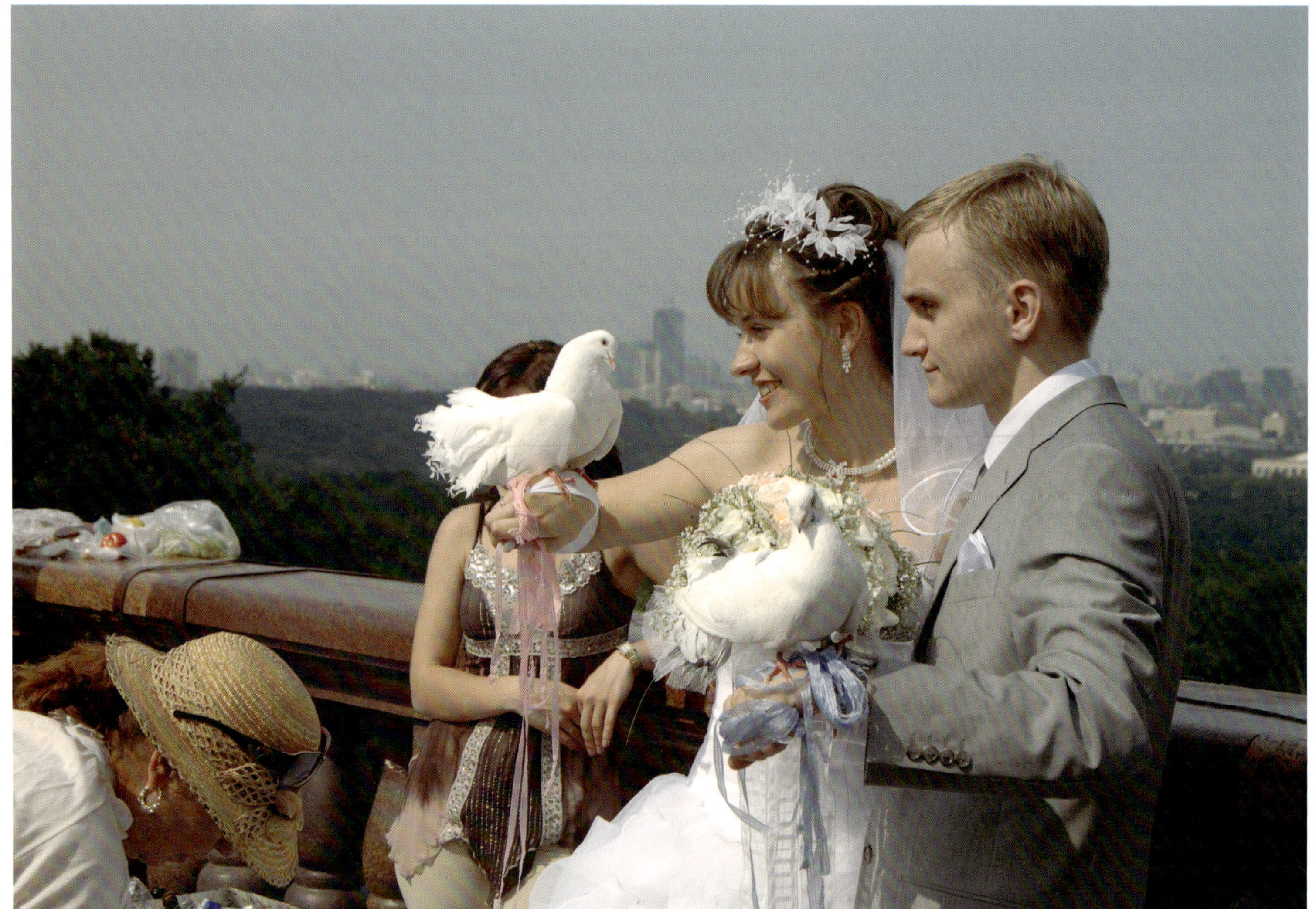

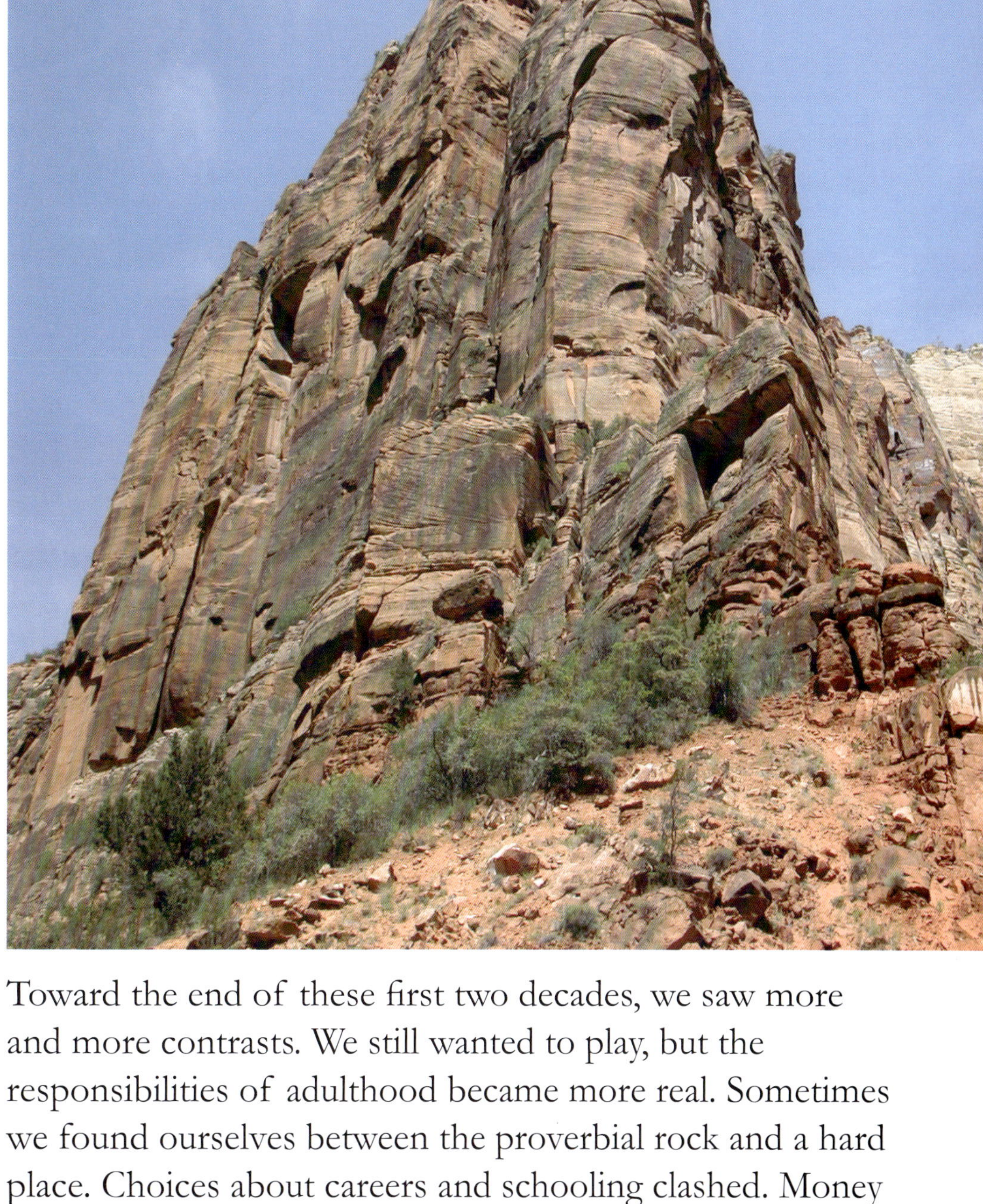

Toward the end of these first two decades, we saw more and more contrasts. We still wanted to play, but the responsibilities of adulthood became more real. Sometimes we found ourselves between the proverbial rock and a hard place. Choices about careers and schooling clashed. Money often came into play with these decisions. For those who had already married, perhaps even had a family, some choices seemed so inevitable that they didn't really seem like choices at all.

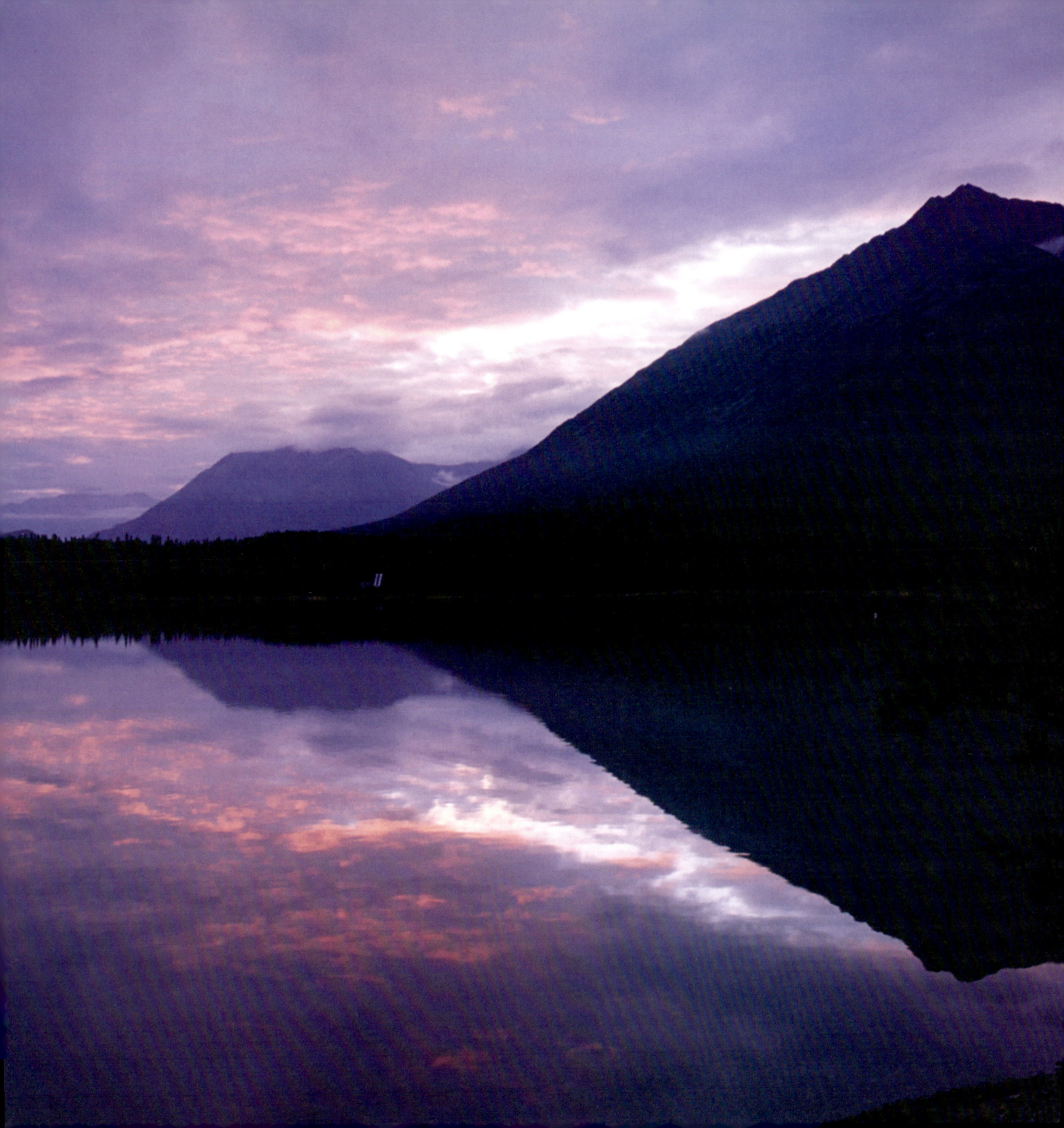

Still, going into our twenties was an exciting time of new beginnings. Like a sunrise, it caught many of us by surprise with the awesomeness of God's presence and the promise of greater things to come.

"There is always one moment in childhood when the door opens and lets the future in."
Graham Greene, *The Power and the Glory*

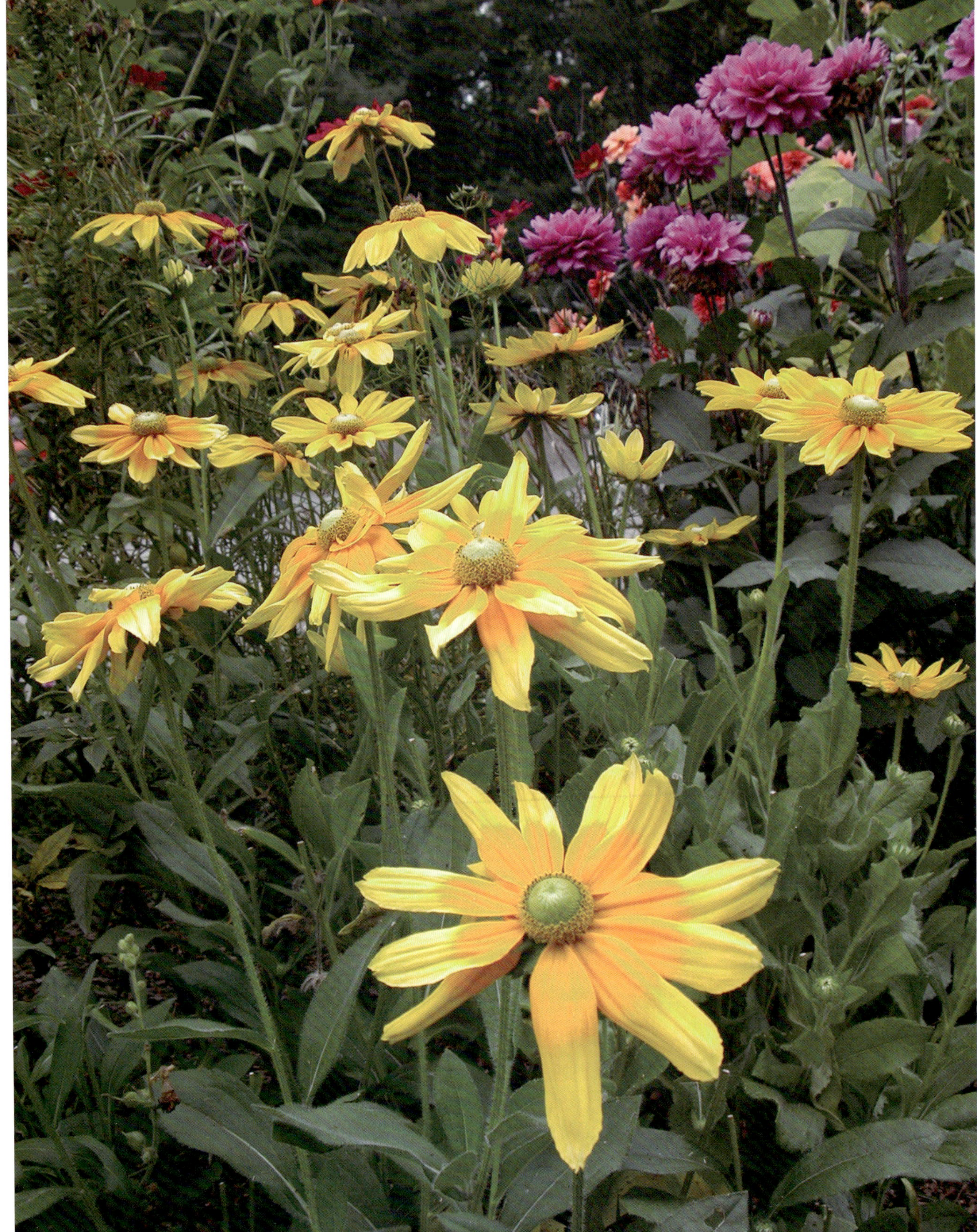

Lesson Learned in Summer

Conquer Fear

There is much to fear in childhood and adolescence. Everything is new. We don't know how things or people work. Most children start out trusting and loving until, or unless, some adult or experience changes that positive outlook.

The majority of parents want good things for their children. Some of the most loving ones have little in the way of material possessions but are rich in the time they spend paying attention to their young ones.

Showing love by being mindful of what children need is a gift every parent can give. Knowing our children well enough to acknowledge their needs means we help them recognize their intrinsic worth without measuring them against our accomplishments, those of their siblings, or anyone else's.

Everyone has a fear of failure. It is a given of the human condition. When children are given the opportunity to make decisions at an early age, they will inevitably make some not-so-good ones. How much better it is when that happens within the confines of a loving, supportive family. It helps ensure that only a minimal sense of worth is lost.

Over-protecting children from errors by not letting them make their own choices does not do them any favors. It simply delays the hard lessons to a later date and increases their dependence on their parents. James Joyce wrote, "A man's errors are his portals of discovery." It's best not to block children's desire and ability to discover.

We fear what we don't understand. We are afraid of appearing foolish. A good exercise is to think through the absolute worst thing that can happen, given the particular circumstances. Then look at that from a logical perspective. What is the statistical likelihood that this awfulness will actually occur?

And if it should happen, what will you do? Often taking it to the extreme makes one begin to cope. And, as experience teaches, most of the things that make us the most anxious never happen.

In this first season of life, when we realize we can face what we most fear and survive, no matter how embarrassed we might be at making a mistake or how heartbroken we are to lose a first love, it strengthens us and helps us develop into survivors.

No one, no matter how smart, how attractive, or how wealthy, escapes life's surprising downturns. Learning and dealing with that reality early on prevents paralysis, when the crises increase in magnitude, as they tend to do as we mature.

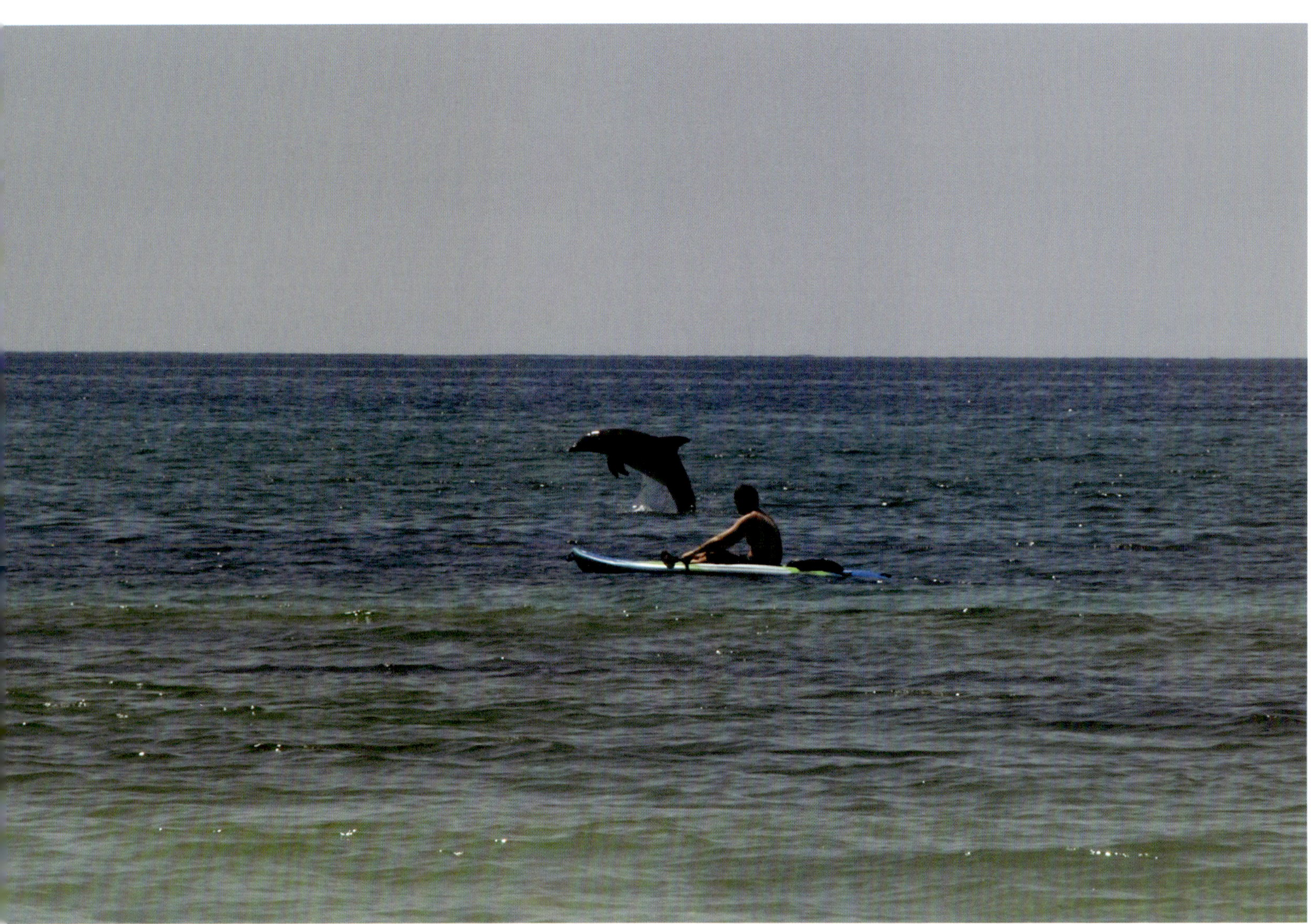

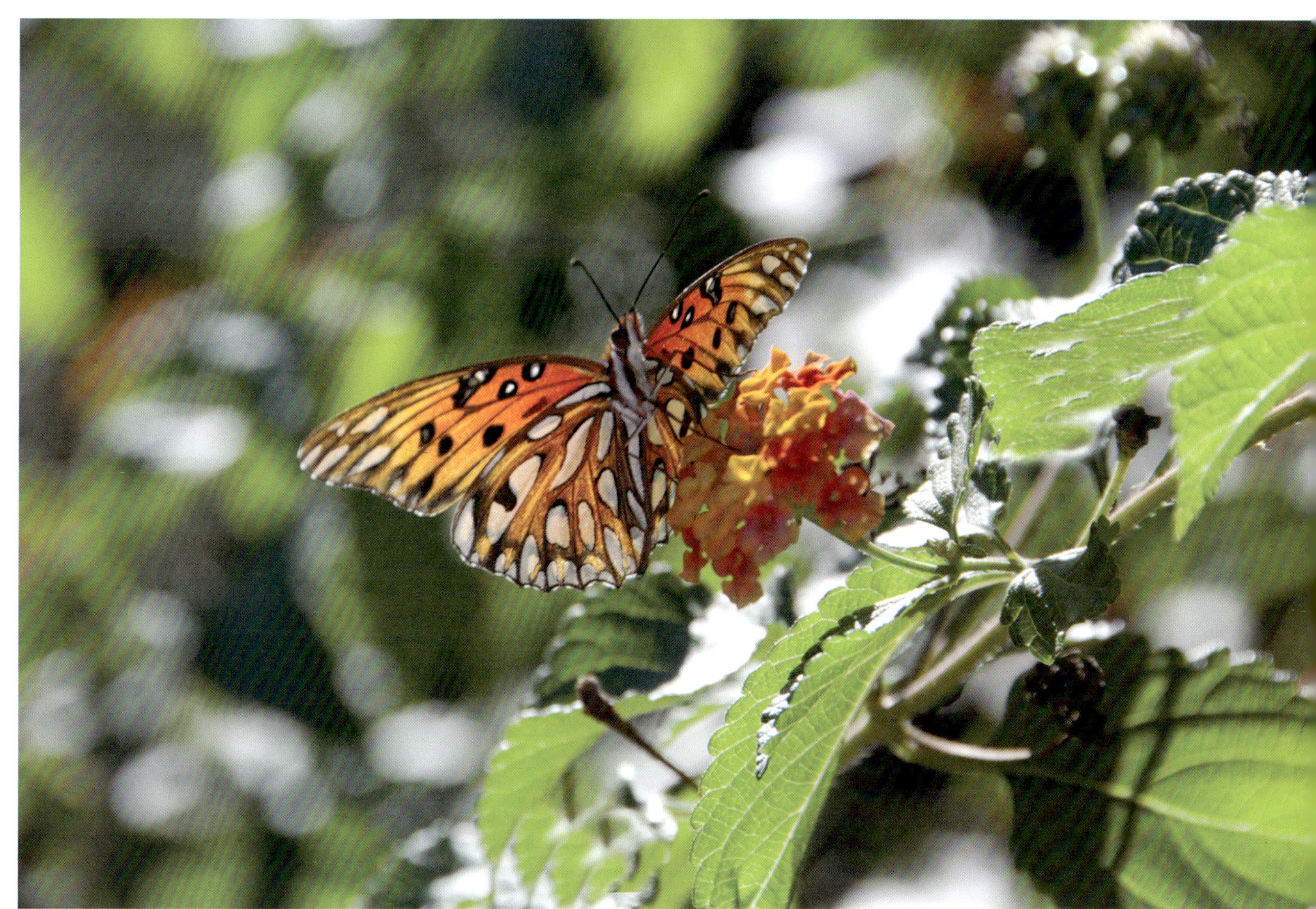

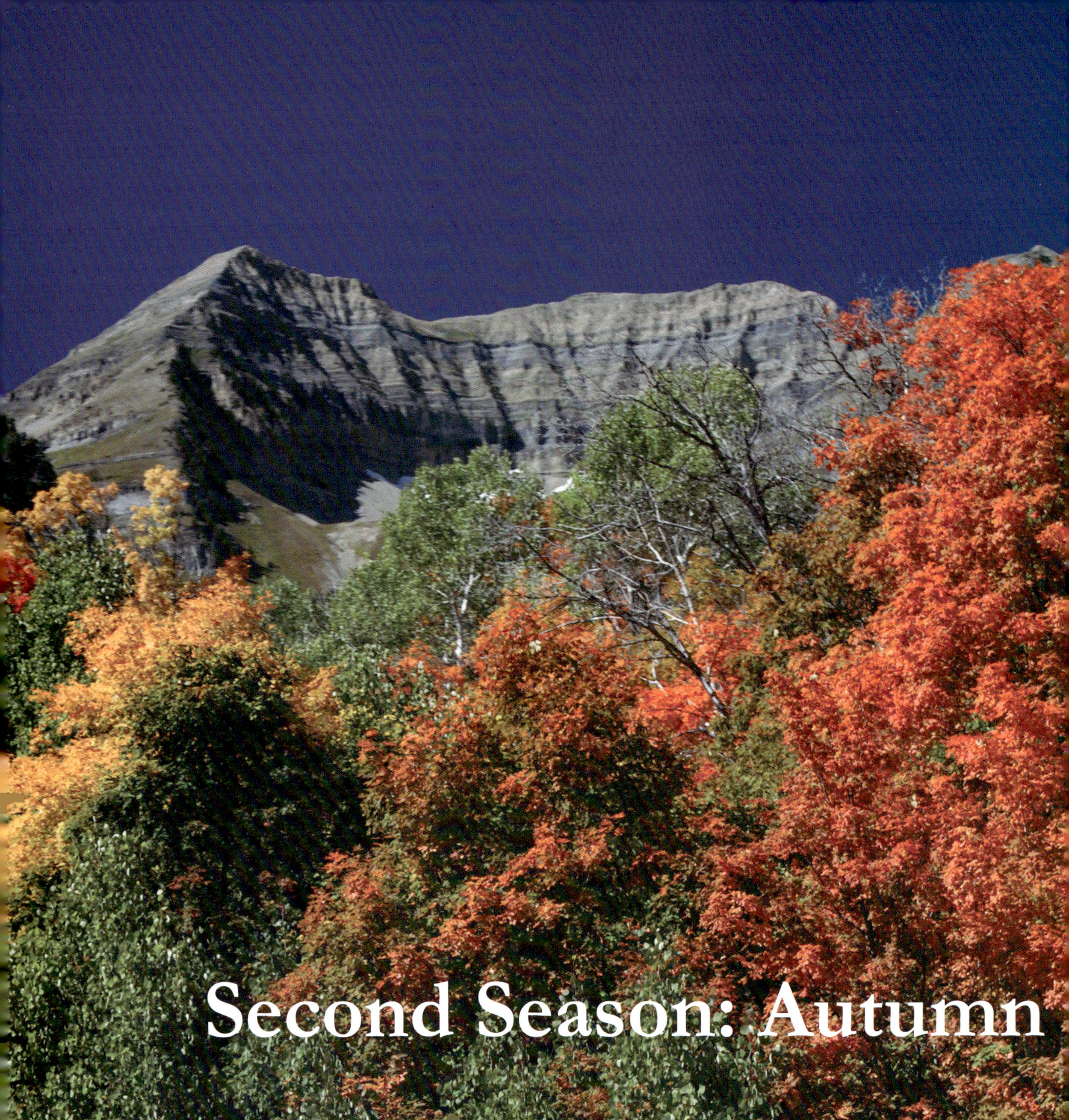

Second Season: Autumn

Song for Autumn

by Mary Oliver

In the deep fall
    don't you imagine the leaves think how
comfortable it will be to touch
    the earth instead of the
nothingess of air and the endless
    freshets of wind? And don't you think
the trees themselves, especially those with mossy
    warm caves, begin to think

of the birds that will come – six, a dozen – to sleep
    inside their bodies? And don't you hear
the goldenrod whispering goodbye,
    the everlasting being crowned with the first
tuffets of snow? The pond
    vanishes, and the white field over which
the fox runs so quickly brings out
    its blue shadows. And the wind pumps its
bellows. And at evening especially,
    the piled firewood shifts a little,
longing to be on its way.

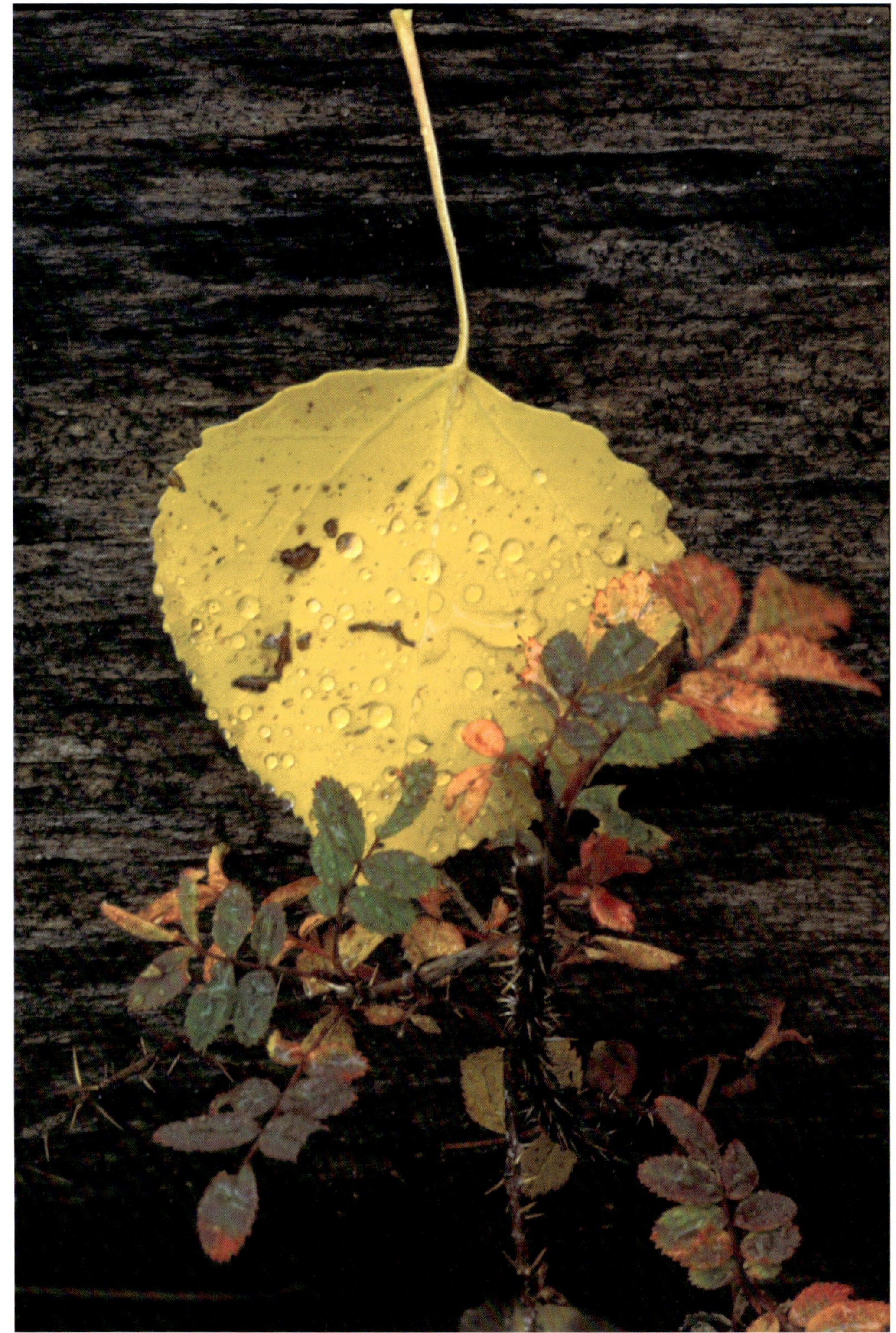

When I was growing up, school never began until after Labor Day. That date not only marked the start of school but also the advent of fall, with a bite to the air and richer colors in leaves and clothing. The focus was on studying hard, trying to master book skills, and broadening our view of the world in the process.

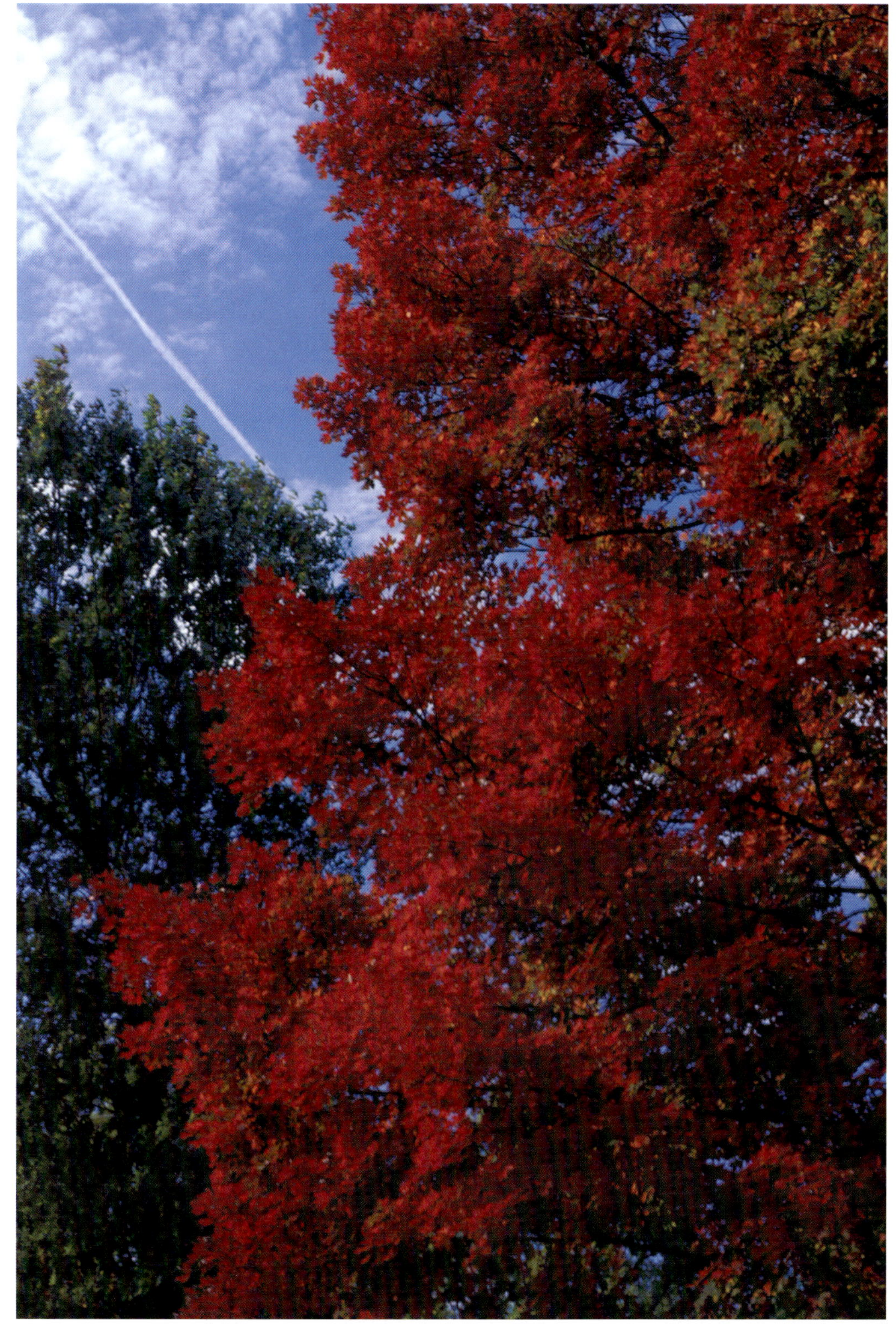

The second quarter of life, ages twenty-one to forty, might be viewed as autumn. It's a very busy time, so much so that many of us forget to savor life's lessons. Most twenty-one-year-olds are soon to set out on their own, if they haven't already done so.

At this age, we look ahead to more schooling, new jobs, first-time spouses, and first-time families. There's a lot of enthusiasm in the early part of this stage, similar to that generated at autumn football and soccer games. Optimism and cheers, a nothing-can-stop-me attitude, help define this season.

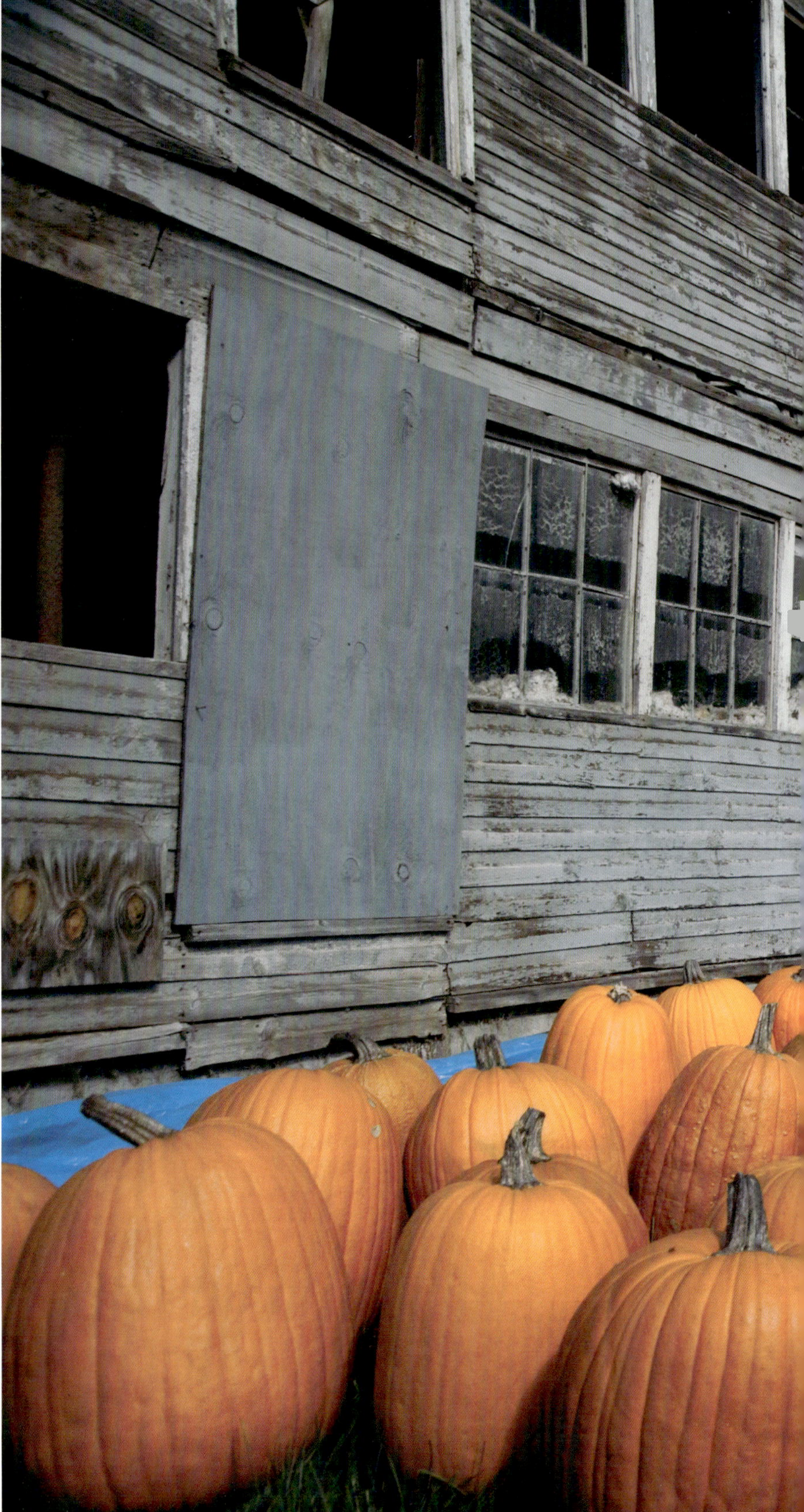

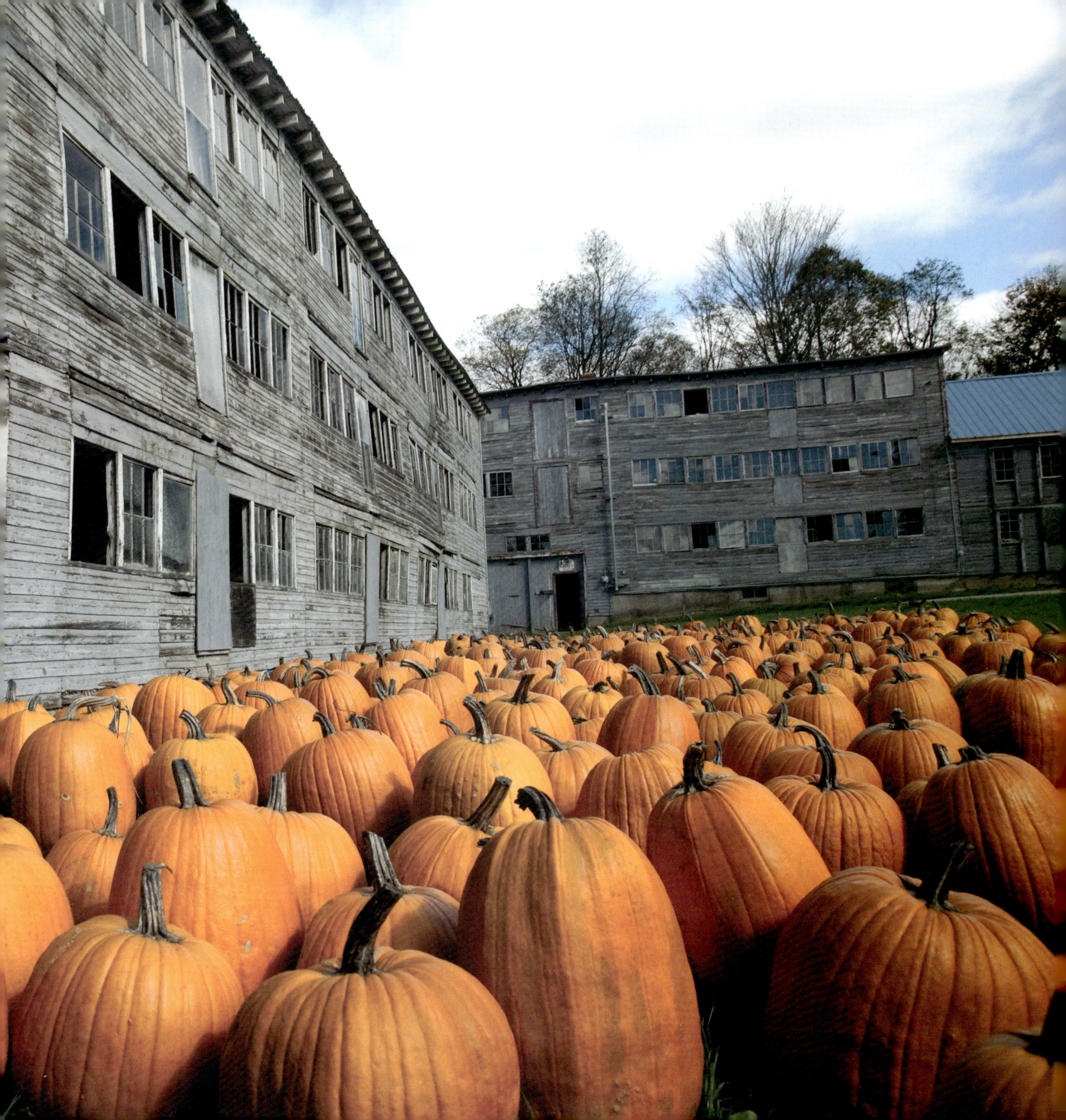

Biking is an appropriate sports metaphor for this phase of life. We now go faster than we did in our first two decades, and we begin to venture further from home. We look for directions and road maps. We take jobs in another part of the country or even the world. Our childlike exuberance sometimes wanes as the reality of bills, diapers, and personal limitations begins to register, but it is exciting to lay the foundation for the rest of adulthood.

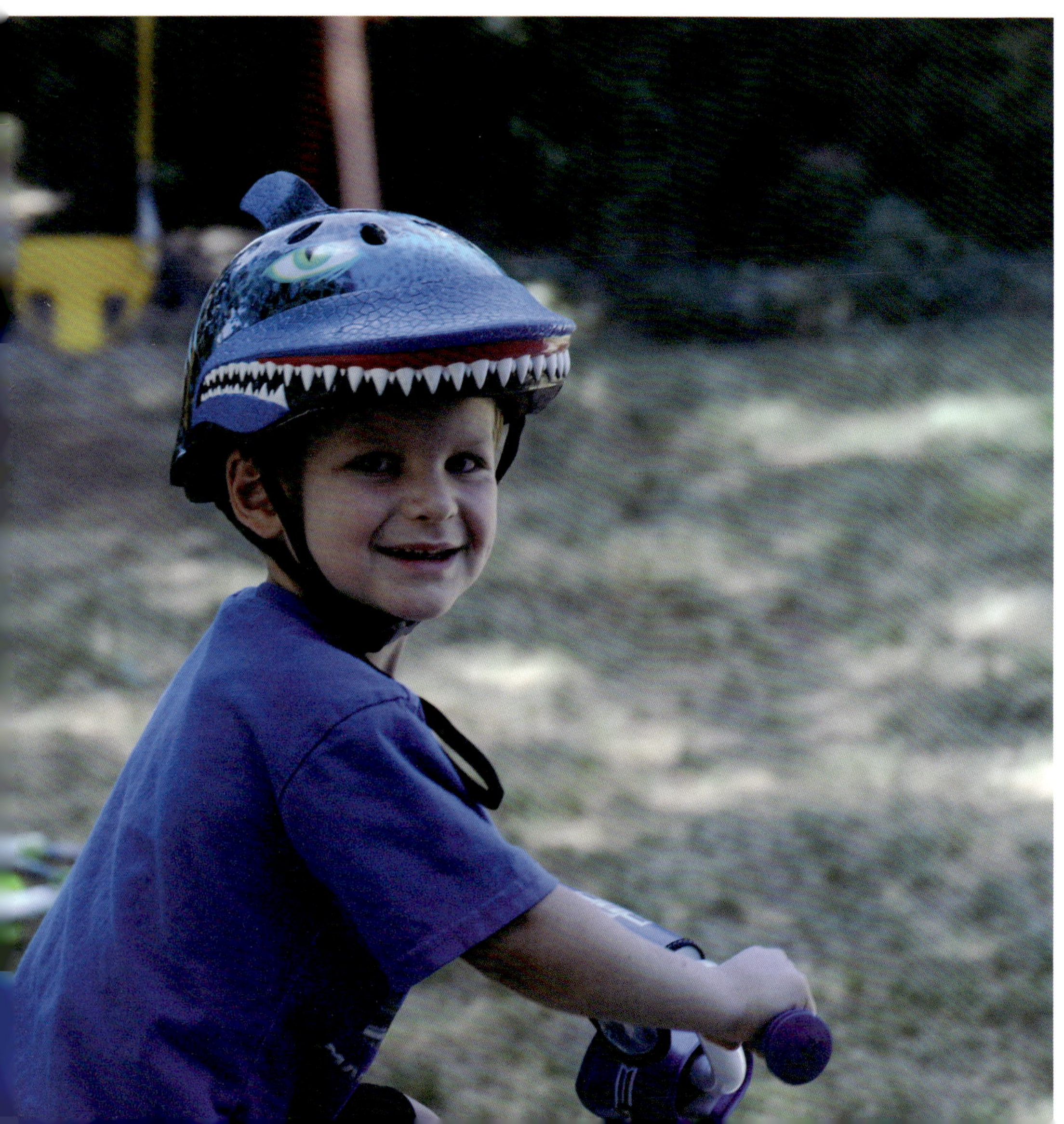

For some, patterns repeat, and we root ourselves in the same places where we grew up and will die, but most of our mobile population becomes comfortable with more transitory places and relations. We stay perhaps five to six years in one town, house, or job, then move on, if not to a bigger place or career, at least to a different one.

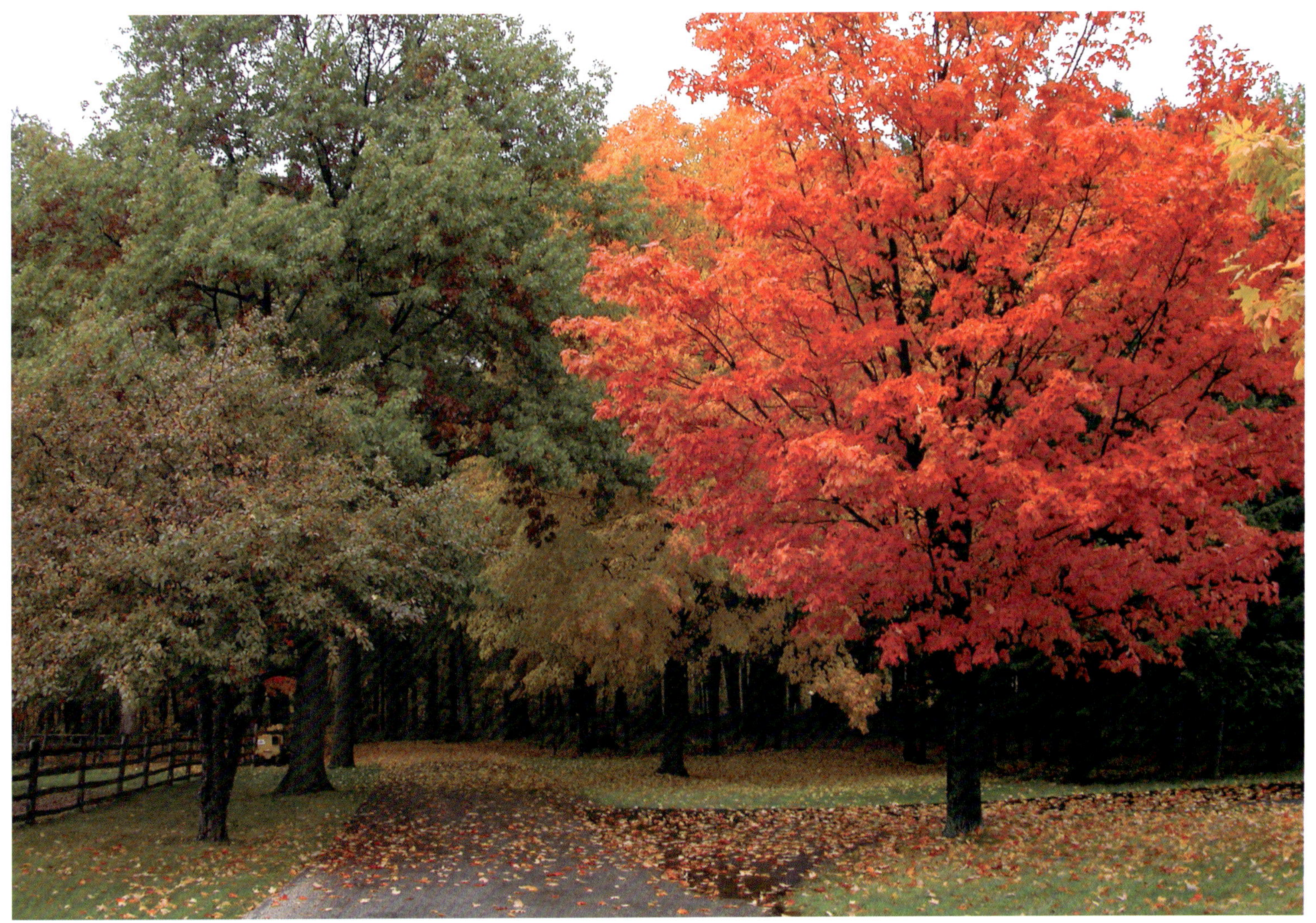

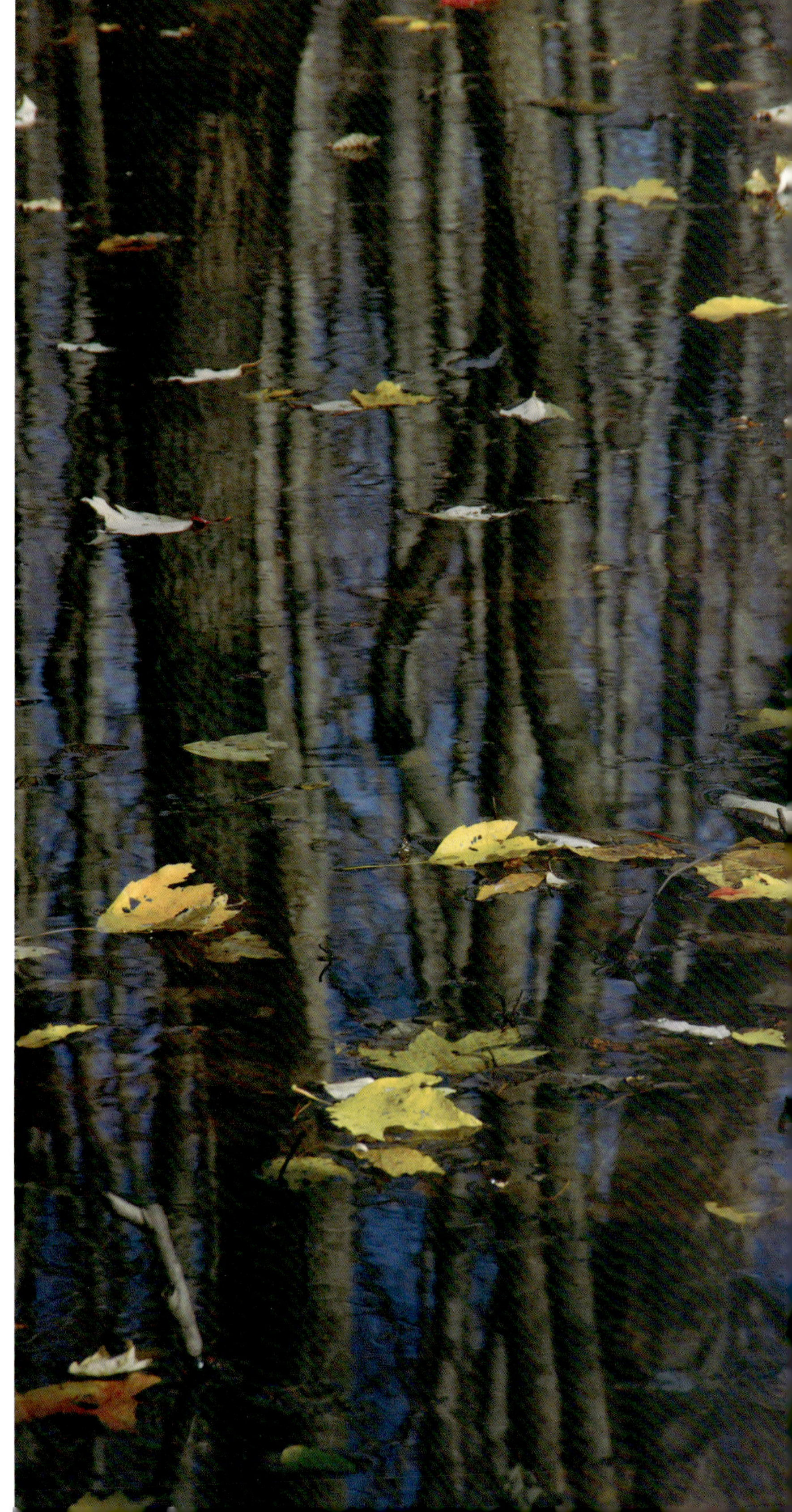

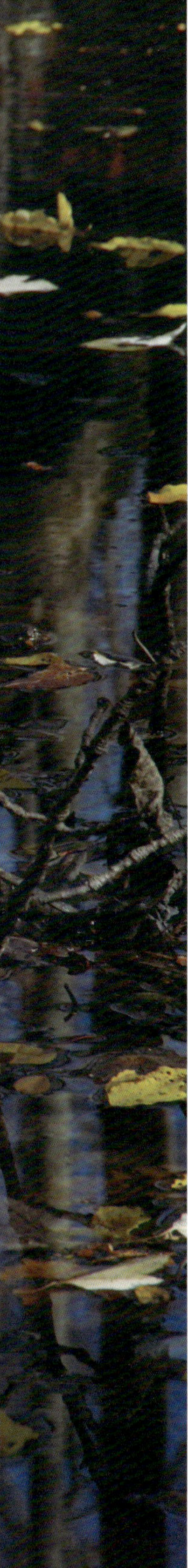

Quiet times are hard to come by as more and more women join men as the primary breadwinners while continuing to run their households and manage their children. Many women wait longer, until they've established careers, to begin their families. However, usually by age forty, even very upwardly mobile women have the children they will bear.

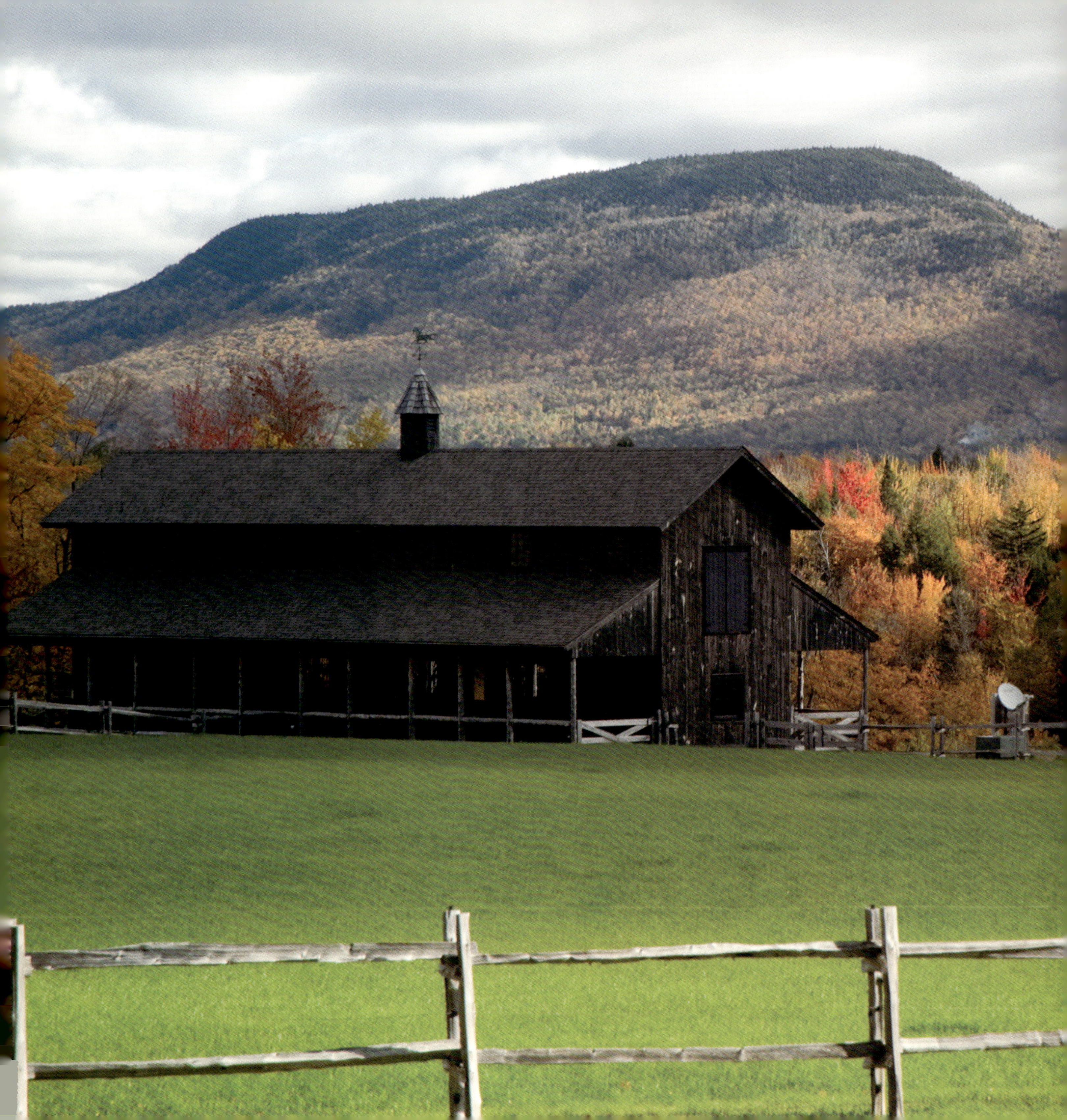

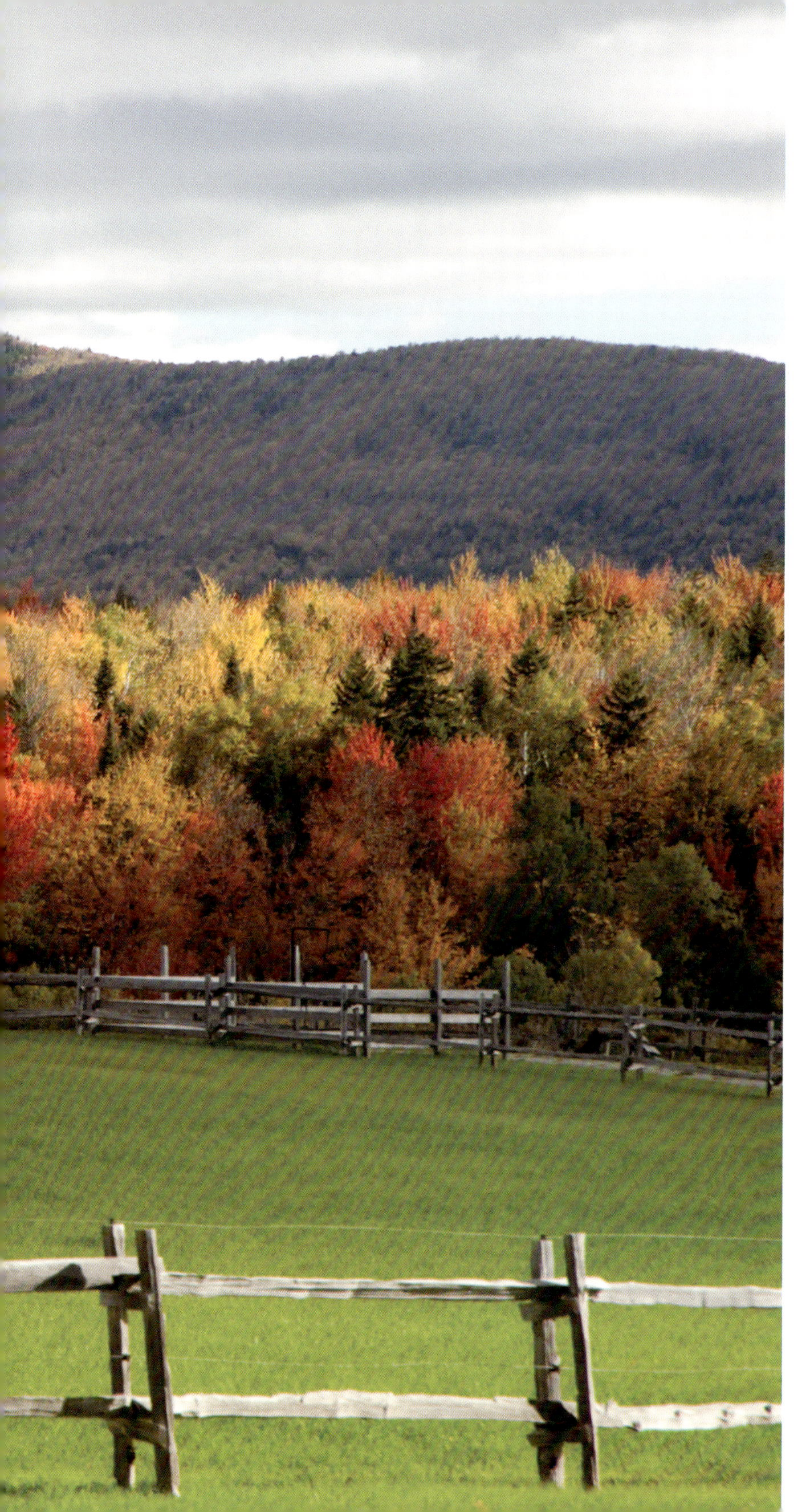

Typically, this season is filled with creating families and learning to balance the responsibilities of family and work. There are lessons and sports for the children as well as – for some – career goals to accomplish. Add to that trying to carve out time for personal development or to engage or reconnect with a partner. Each week is a balancing act.

It is easy for both husbands and wives to feel lost in the shuffle and to miss seeing the forest for the trees. So much of daily life is spent worrying about the future: will complicated schedules align? Or lamenting the past: I couldn't get that report in on time because a child became ill or a spouse needed extra attention.

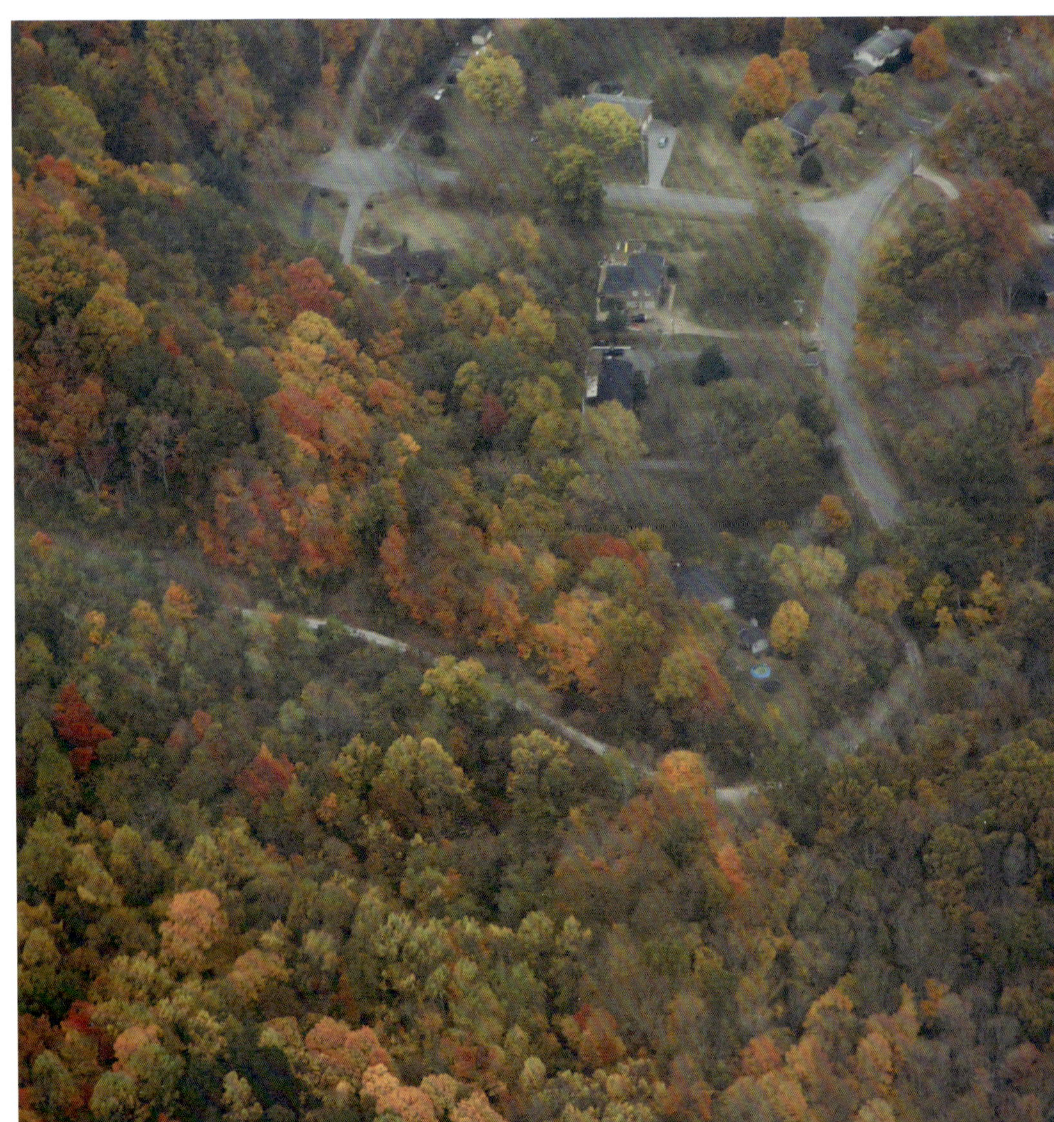

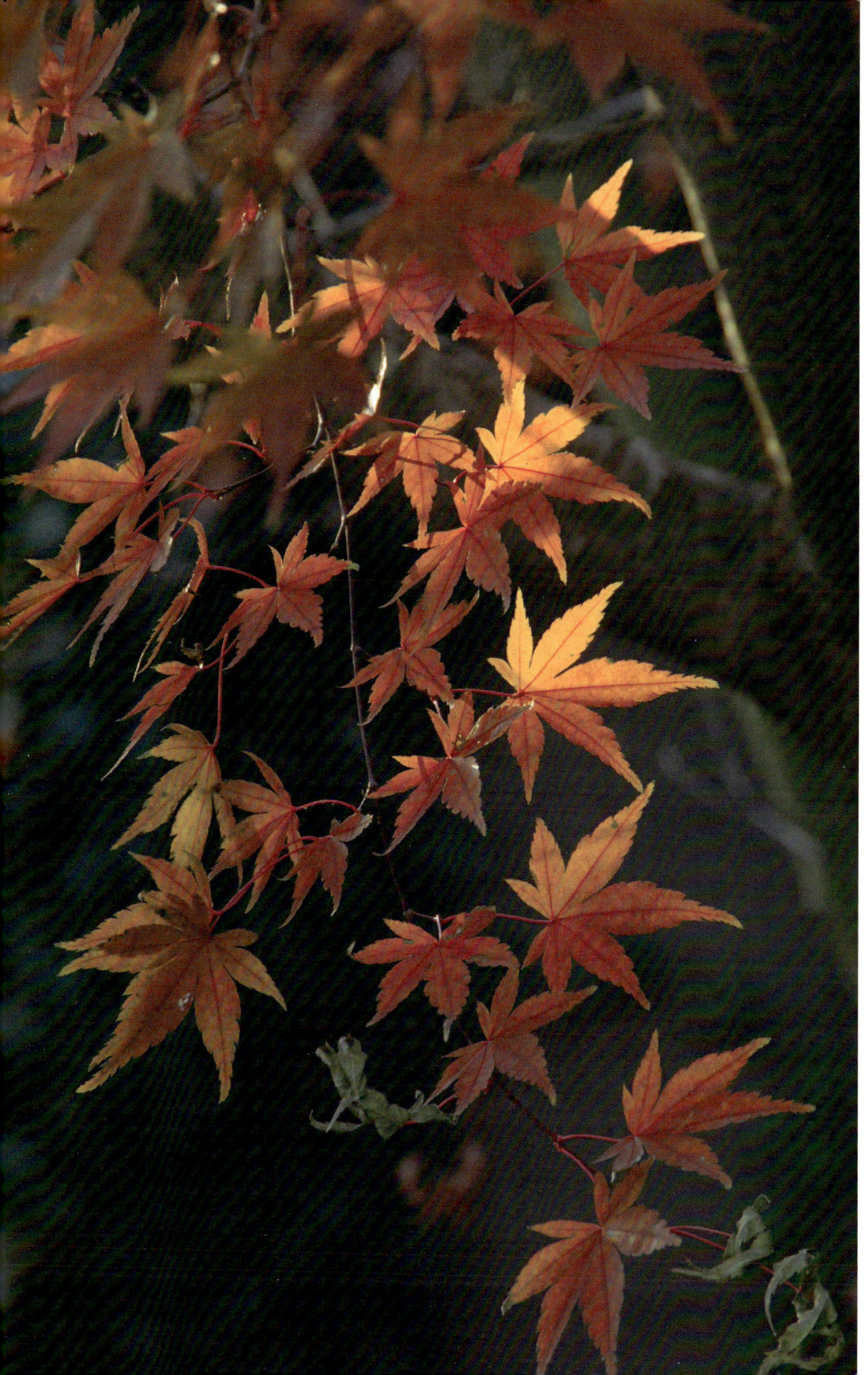

It seems we never live in the moment we are in. We plan for when that moment will come around again, when we aren't so busy, but it seldom does.

There are some shining, incredible times that stand out in our memories. The pride we feel when one of our children is totally motivated on his or her own to do something good for someone else. A walk in the woods with our partner. Sharing the delights of an early fall. A compliment from a co-worker about a project we worked long and hard on.

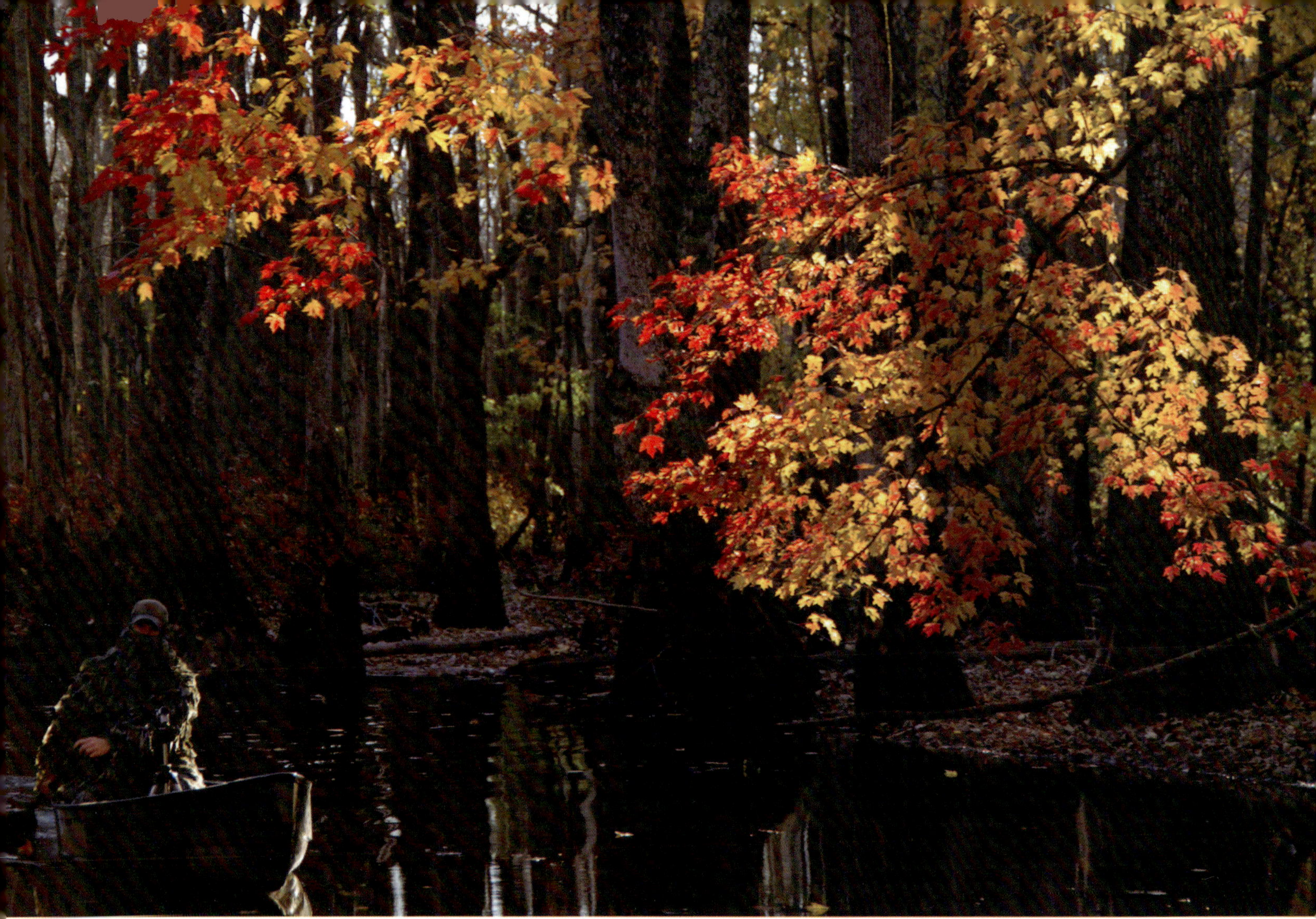

Being alone is rather difficult to arrange. We feel guilty when we try because it means putting ourselves above others, yet our souls cry out for respite. Whenever we do make the break for a few hours or a day, we feel better, refreshed, capable of continuing. Yet every time we try to do this, we face the same inner struggle. Why do we not see that this is a necessary part of caring for ourselves?

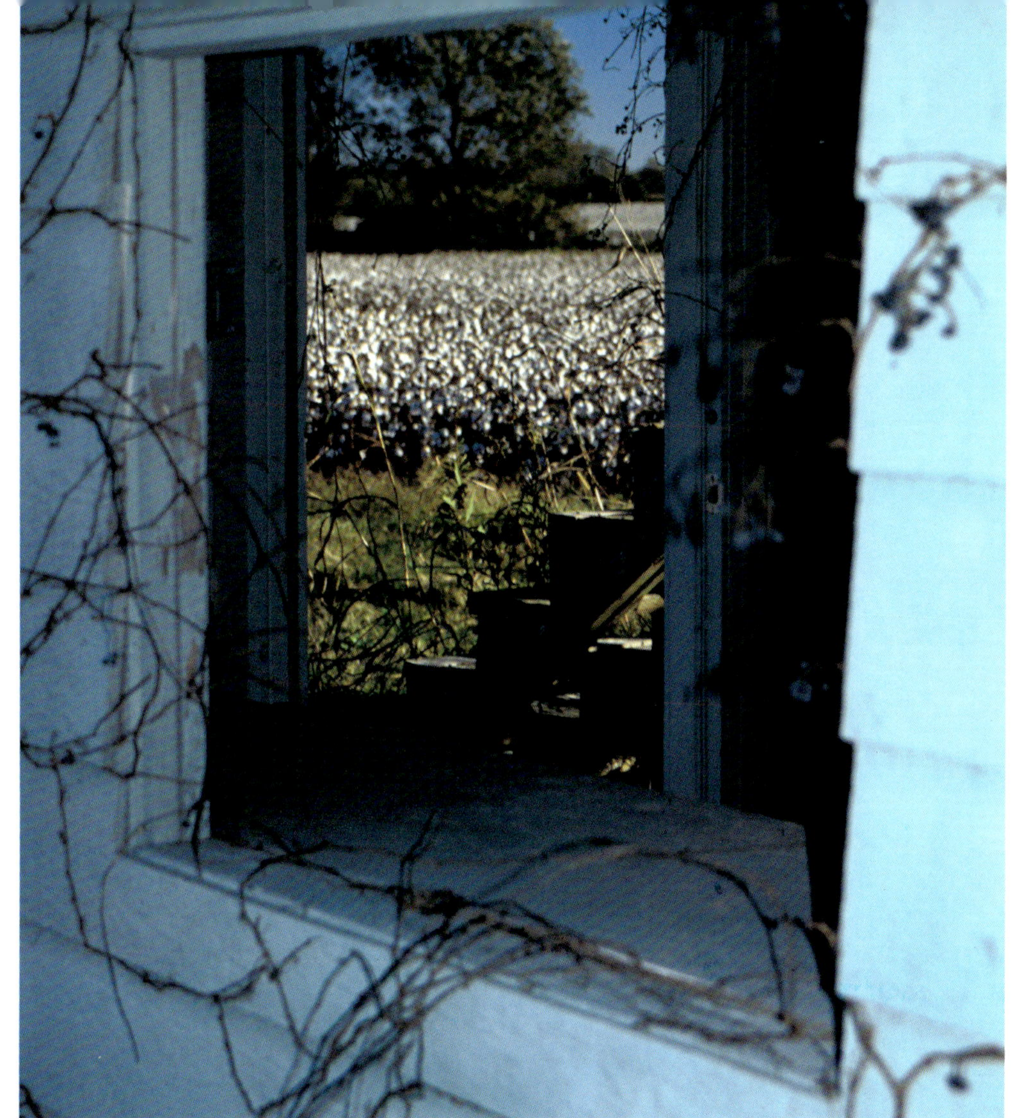

No matter how or where we grew up, we begin to look into our pasts to explore our roots. Perhaps it comes with having children or entering the halfway point of life that creates in us a curiosity about our ancestors, their way of life, and their similarities and differences to our own.

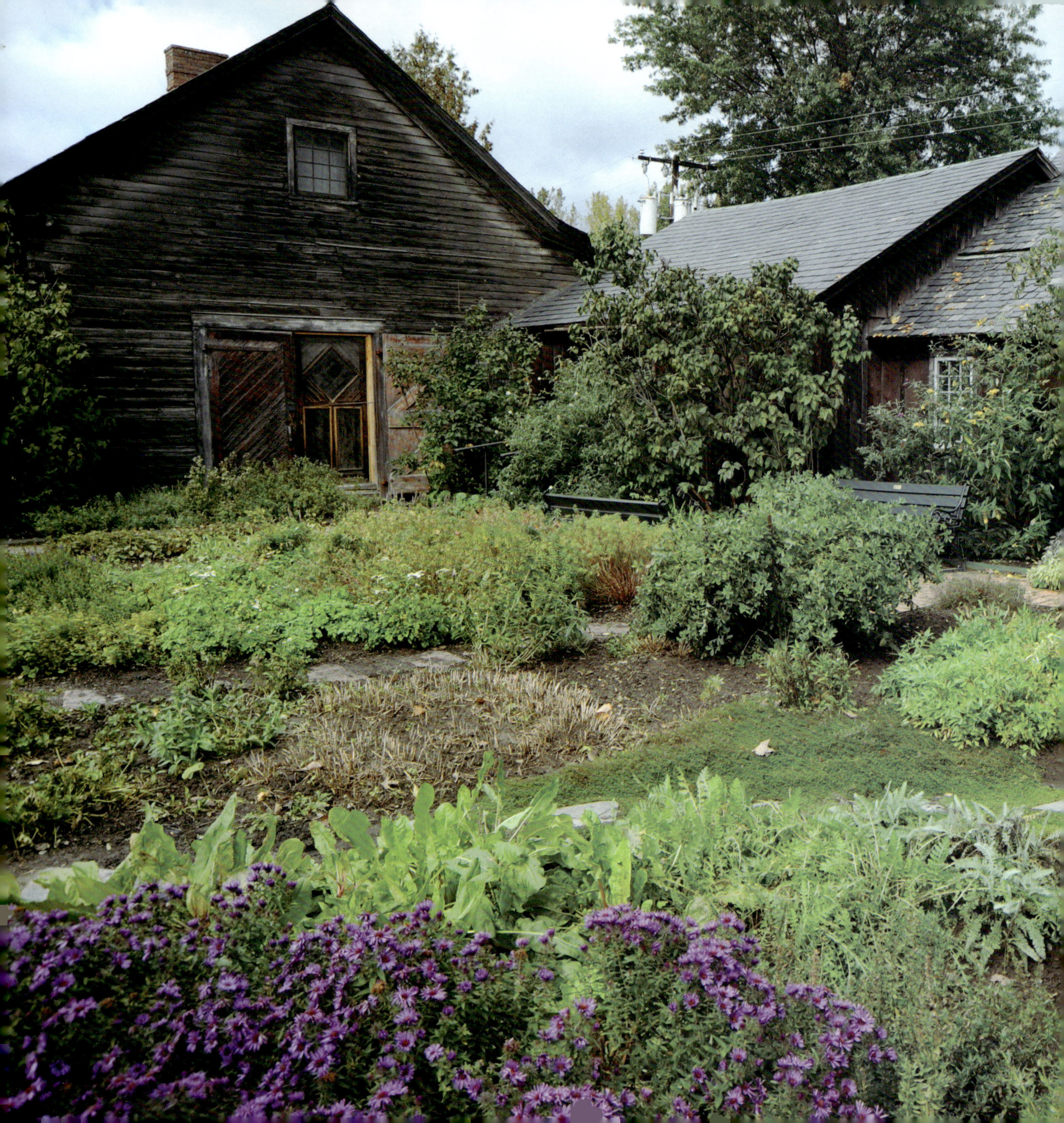

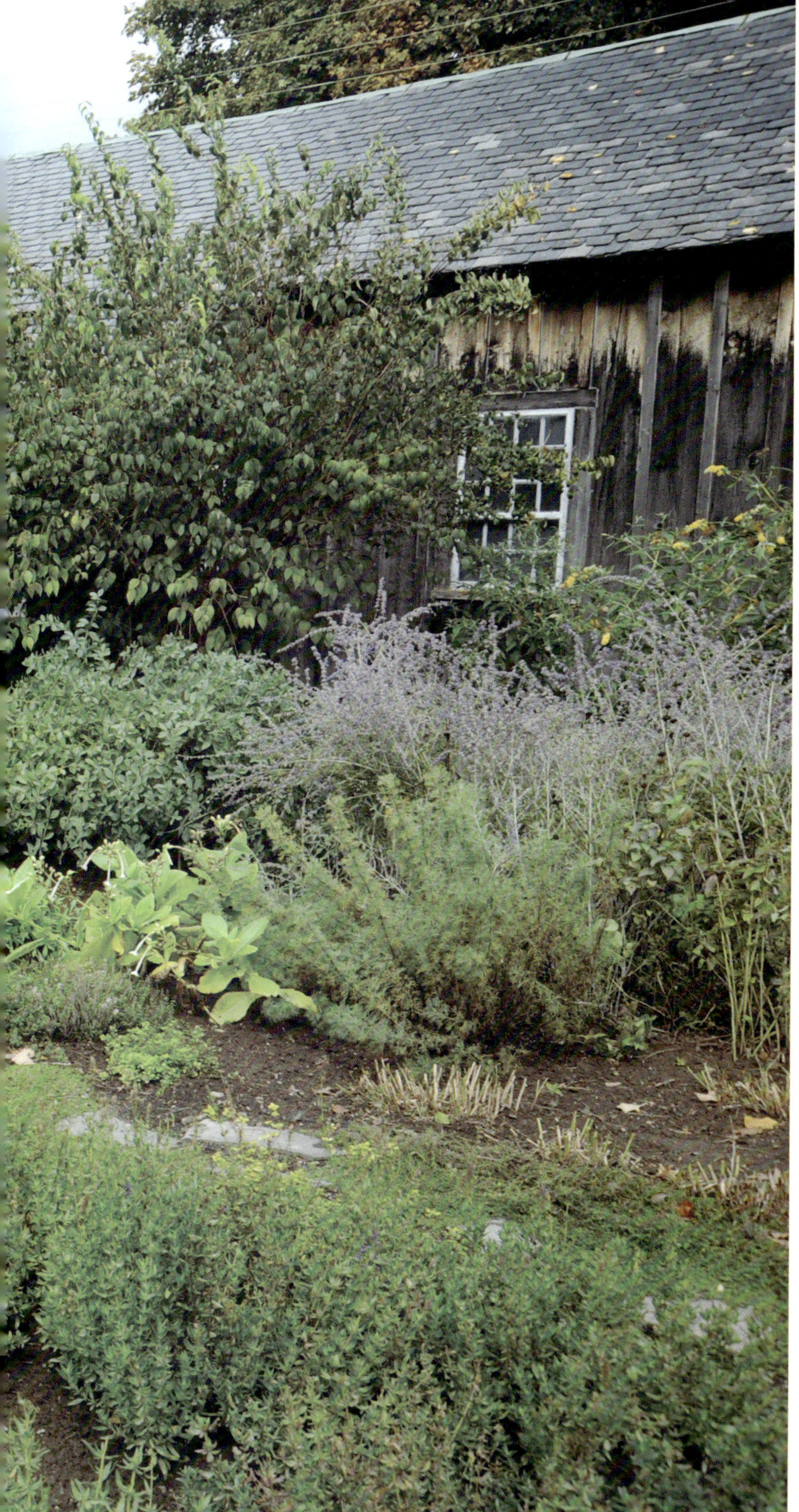

My grandmother, my mother's mother, for whom I was named, lived on a farm out in the country most of her life. Maybe that's why, as a young parent, I kept a little garden plot off and on. It seemed magical to be able to plant seeds and harvest food in my own backyard.

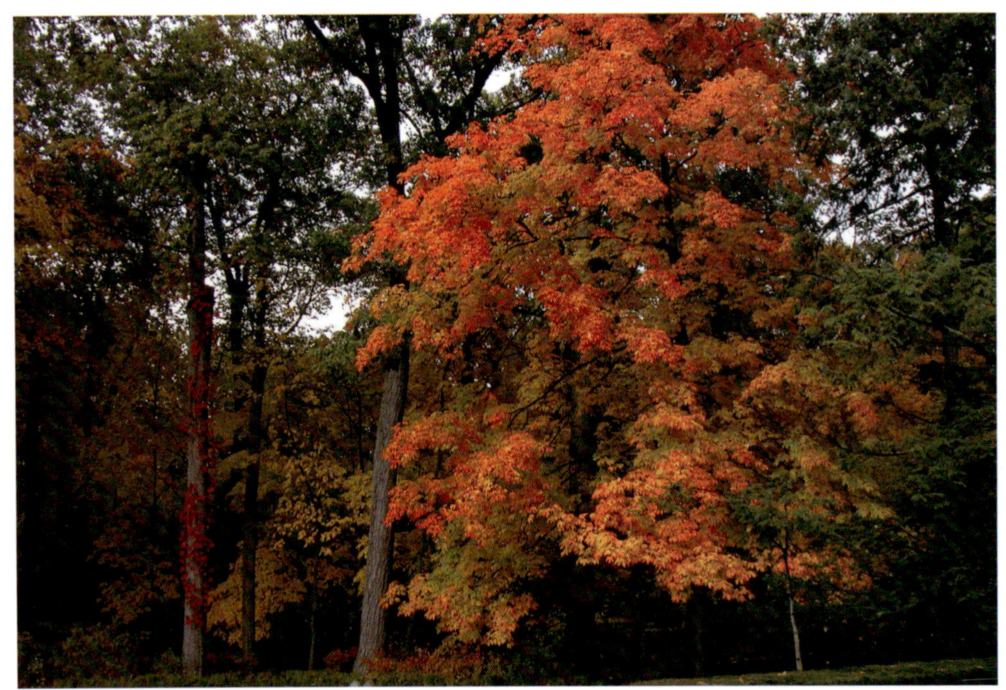

Notice how autumn comes to some trees a leaf at a time, gradually rather than all of a sudden? Fluttering next to one another are green leaves tinged with orange, leaves that are half orange, and leaves that blaze orange all over.

Middle age creeps in the same way. Am I young or am I old when traits of each extreme lie side by side? Some days, I feel youth in my bones; other days, I feel fully middle aged.

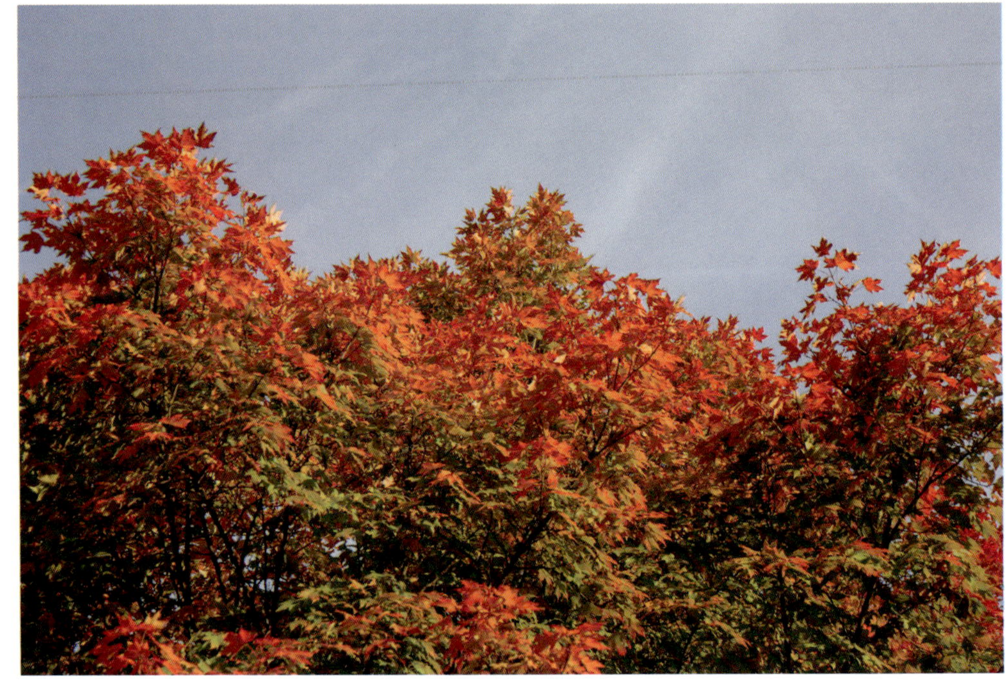

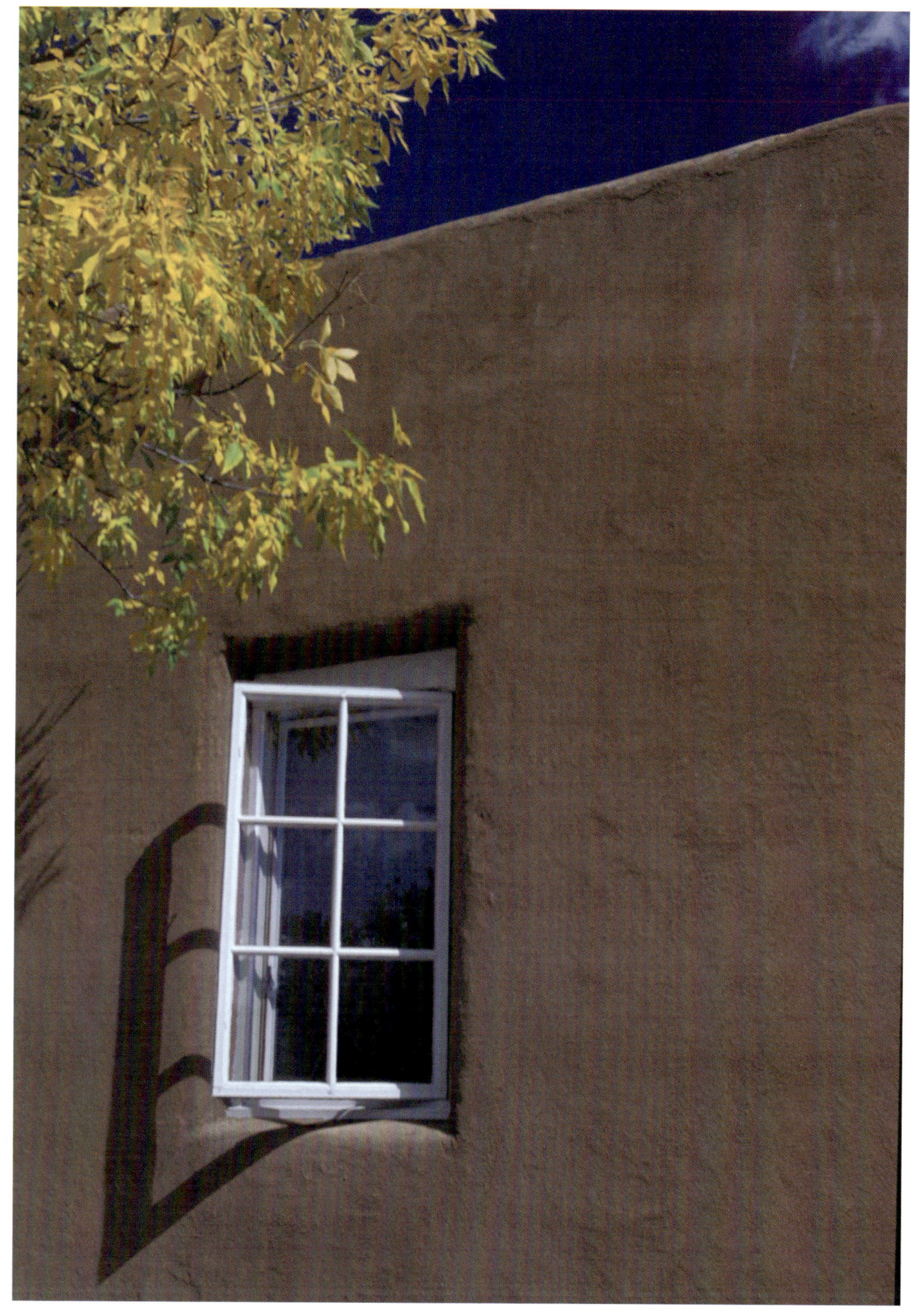

We've managed to protect ourselves from so much of nature in our high-tech world. We heat and air condition our homes, our cars, and our offices and perhaps breathe fresh air for only a handful of minutes each day. Thus, an open window is almost a sign of rebellion, a reaching out, perhaps unconsciously, for freedom and space.

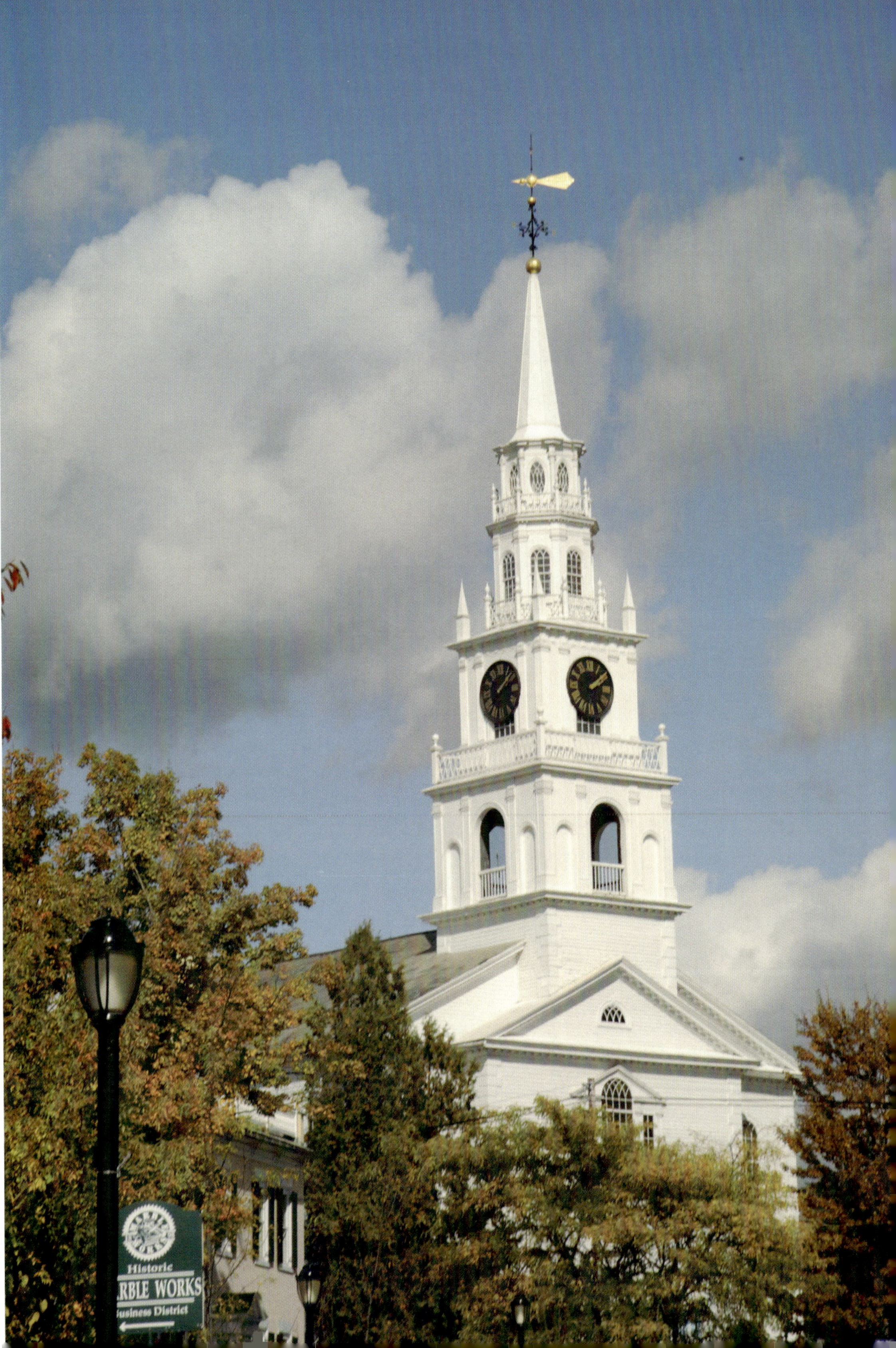
Historic

Midway through life, it is fitting that we find ourselves looking up for help, for inspiration, with gratitude that we are still here, still seeking, still trying to do the right thing for ourselves and all those friends and loved ones around us.

"We don't understand life any better at forty than at twenty, but we know it and admit it."
Jules Renard, *Journal*

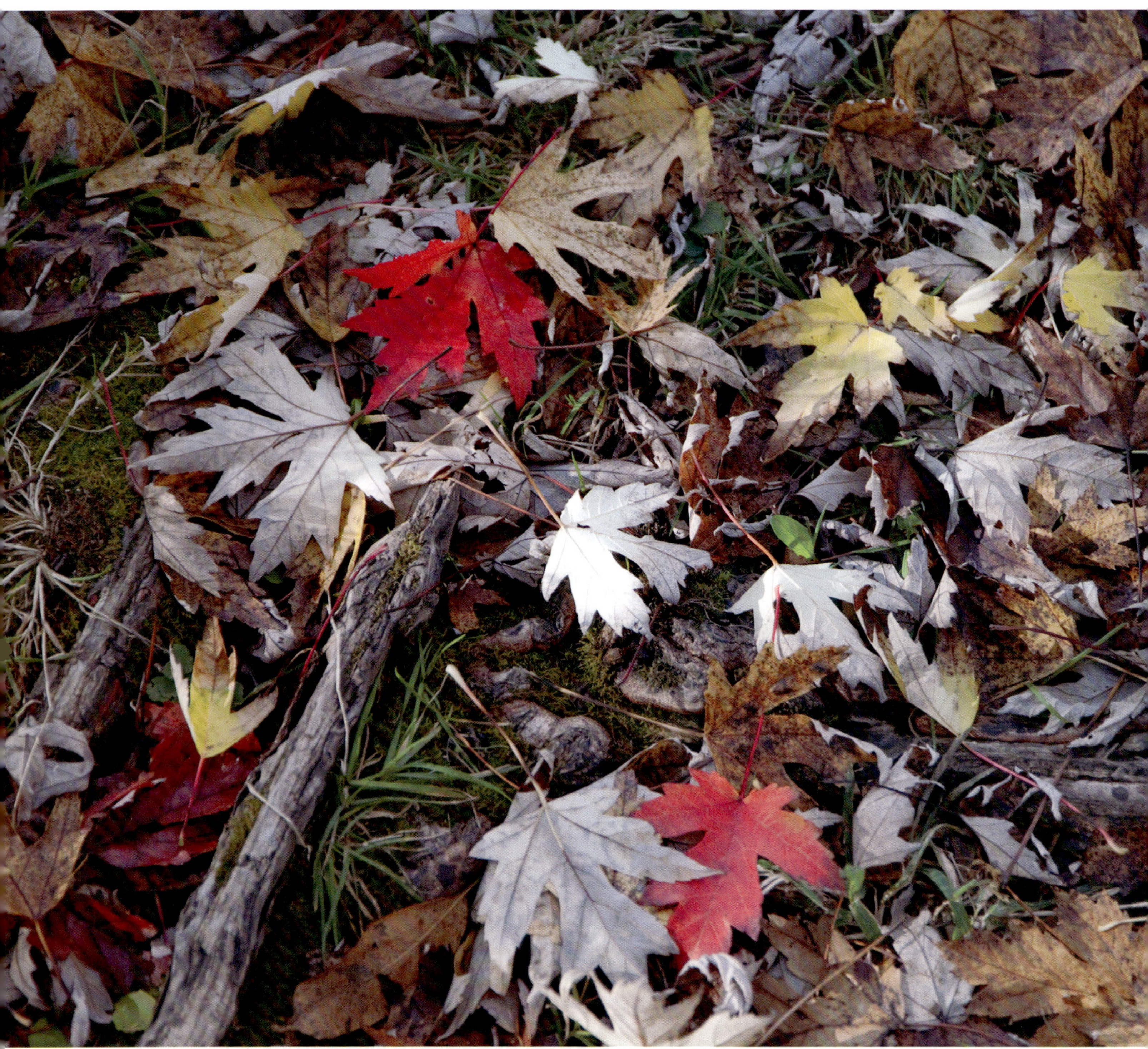

Lesson Learned in Autumn

Continue Learning

Once we have graduated from high school and then perhaps from a community college, a four-year institution, or beyond, most of us think, "Enough! I want to live life, not spend all my time preparing for it!"

Some swear they will never study again, yet in this age of information, the need, if not the desire, for life-long learning is critical. Thanks to Google, quick answers to simple questions are literally at our fingertips.

Serious answers require more effort. No matter what career path we choose, there is much to learn: about the subject itself, about best practices, and about how to improve our memories, our presentation skills, or our salesmanship. The list for growth is limited only by our imaginations and our capacity to learn new things.

Reading and studying can make us citizens of the world, not just of Cincinnati or Chicago. We may want to take a break from the books once we have a degree in hand, but let it be a short vacation, not a permanent trip.

In addition to continuing to learn in order to progress in our avocations and careers, if we are paying attention, we are learning about others by developing the habit of active listening. Too often we half-listen as we think of what we'll say next. At other times, we're too busy making literal or figurative to-do lists to actively listen to those around us.

If we thought this day were the last one we'd have to hear what was important to our spouse or our child, wouldn't we focus intently and try to hear what wasn't being verbalized? Moving through the seasons helps us prioritize, and we finally understand that nothing is more important than the loving and caring relationships we build with family and friends.

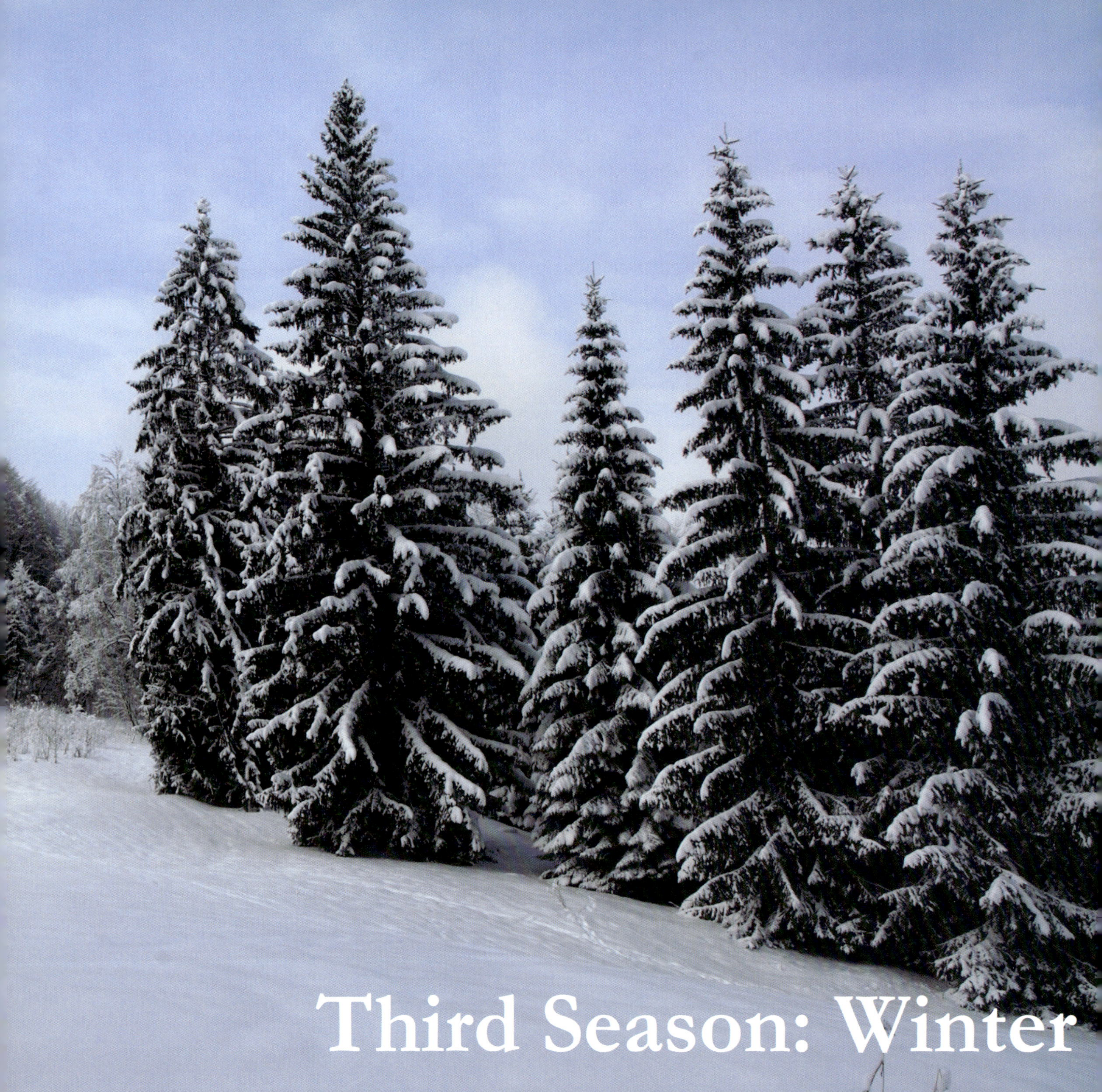

Third Season: Winter

White Heron Rises Over Blackwater

by Mary Oliver

I wonder
what it is
that I will accomplish
today

if anything
can be called
that marvelous word.
It won't be

my kind of work,
which is only putting
words on a page,
the pencil

haltingly calling up
the light of the world,
yet nothing appearing on paper
half as bright

as the mockingbird's
verbal hilarity
in the still unleafed shrub
in the churchyard –

or the white heron
rising
over the swamp
and the darkness,

his yellow eyes
and broad wings wearing
the light of the world
in the light of the world –

ah, yes, I see him.
He is exactly
the poem
I wanted to write.

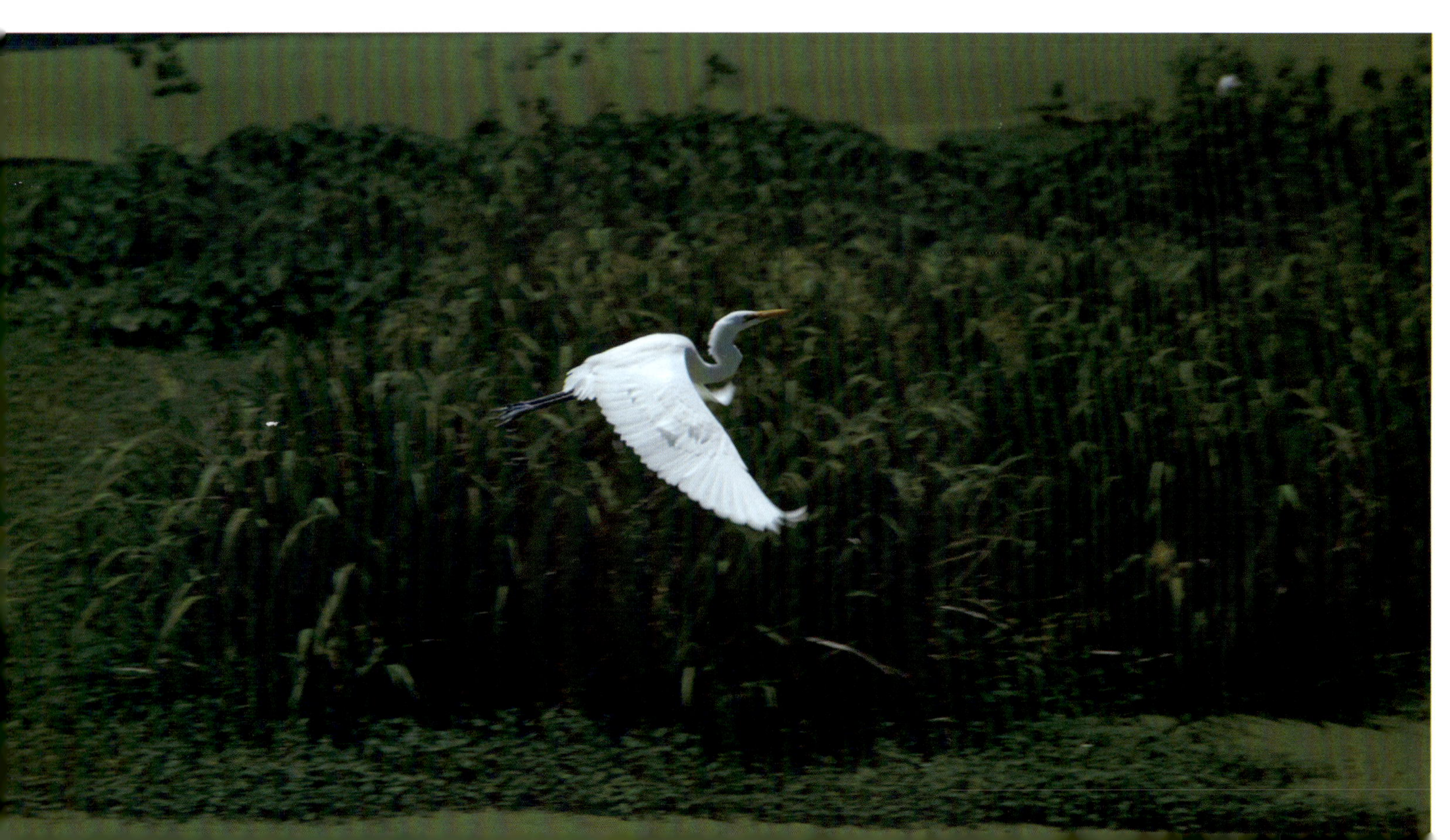

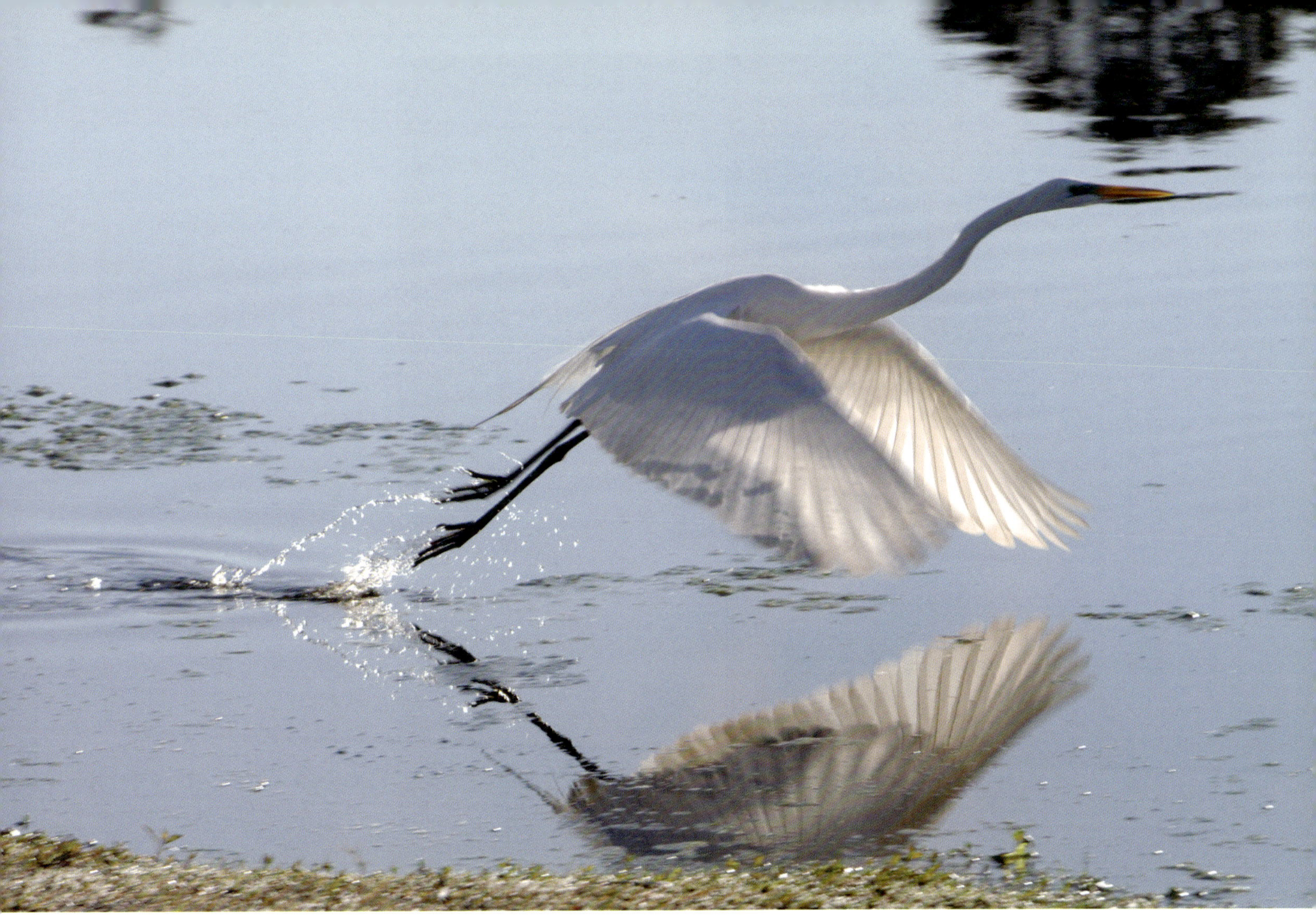

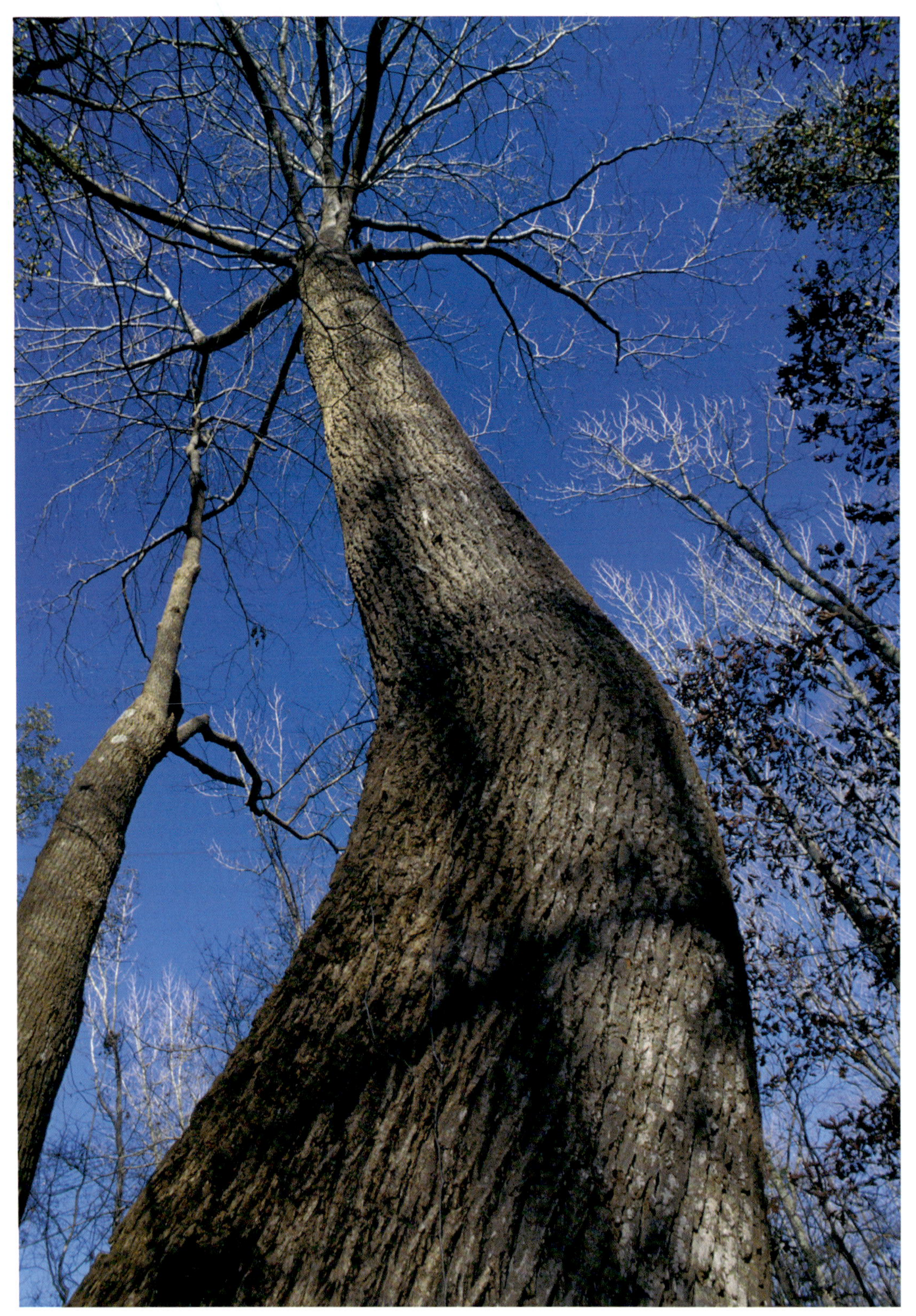

Here's where it can get tough. Winter is often a time of dying. From ages forty-one to sixty, some people just wish that they could. It would simplify their lives. Unfortunately, a few friends and acquaintances have already done so.

This often seems a barren time. Careers end, often preceded by marriages. Parents live far away and are out of touch or, on the contrary, are dying or in need of help. We may experience both the joys and challenges of having an elderly parent come live with us.

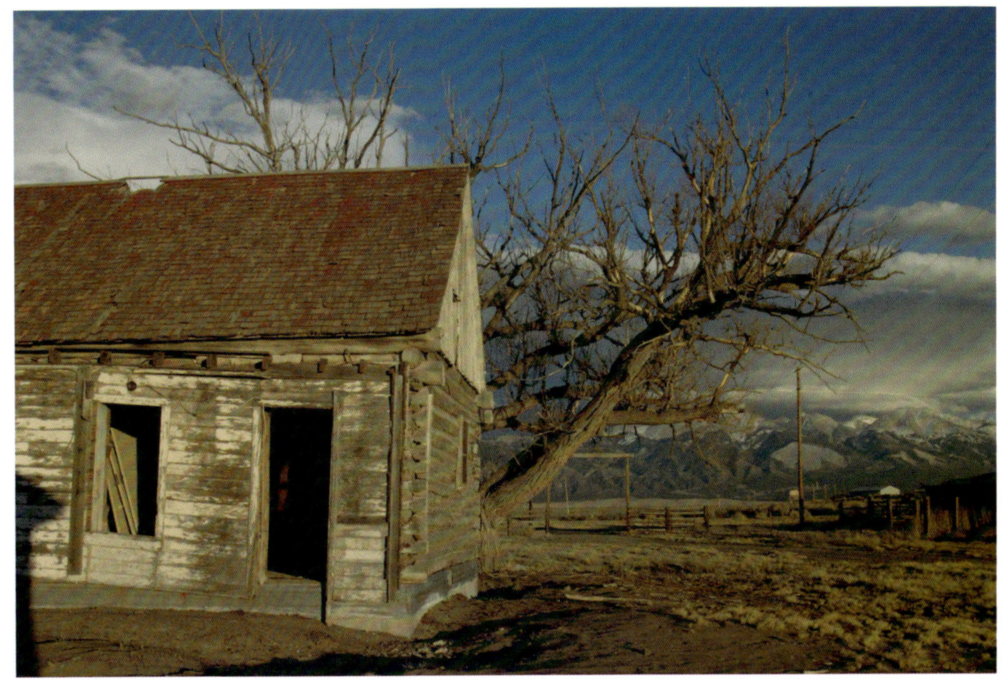

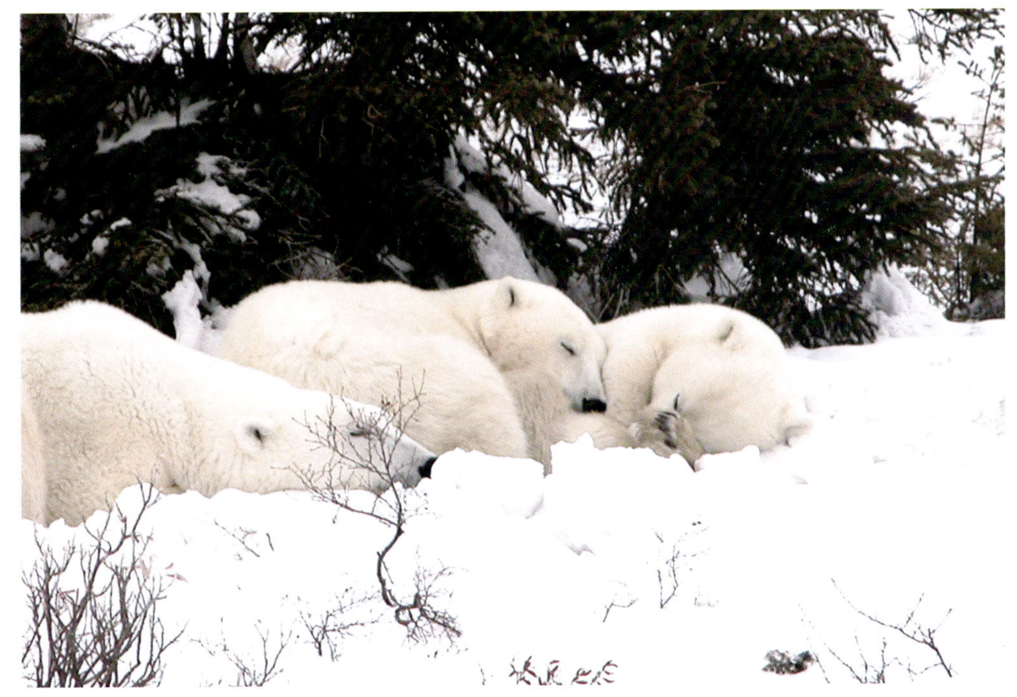

We truly are the sandwich generation, the one that serves as the bridge from the Greatest Generation to Gen X and Gen Y. Our children either move out of the house or return, perhaps with children of their own in tow, adding another layer of direct responsibility.

Consequently, some households consist of three generations as they did a hundred years ago. Sometimes this is the only way families can make ends meet.

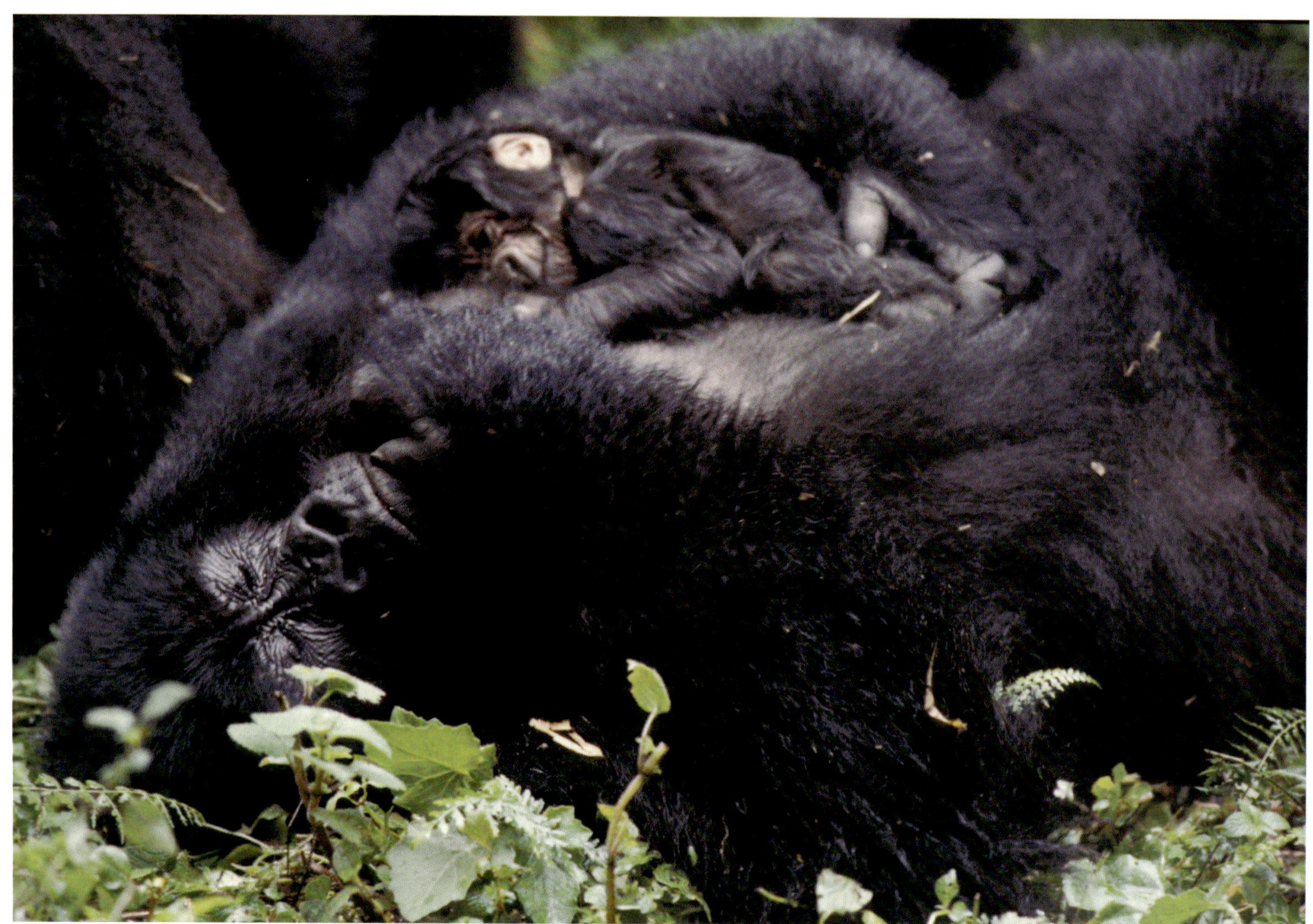

Wisdom comes at a price, usually through some of life's most difficult lessons, yet Americans are their most productive during this season. And, some would say, their most stressed.

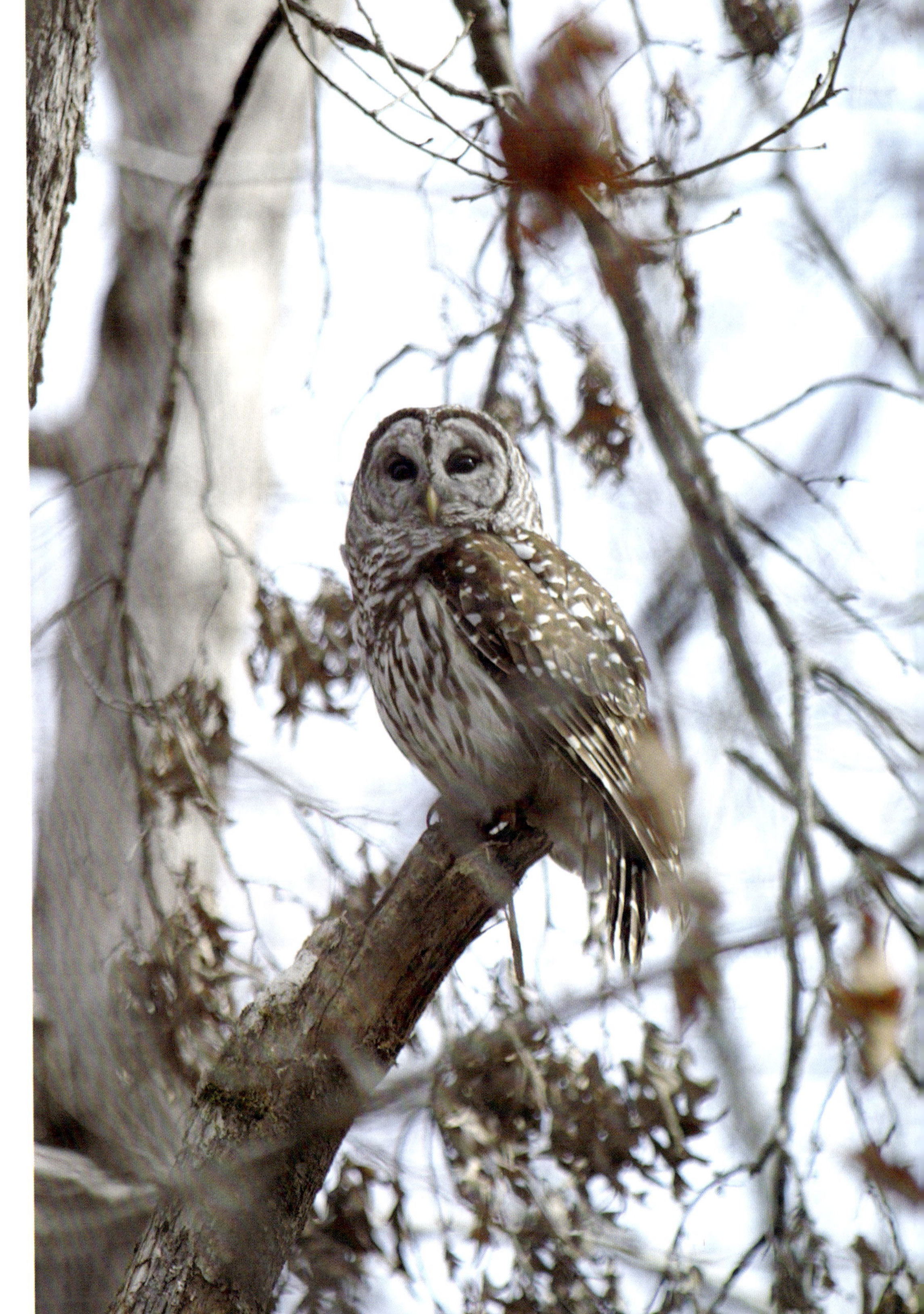

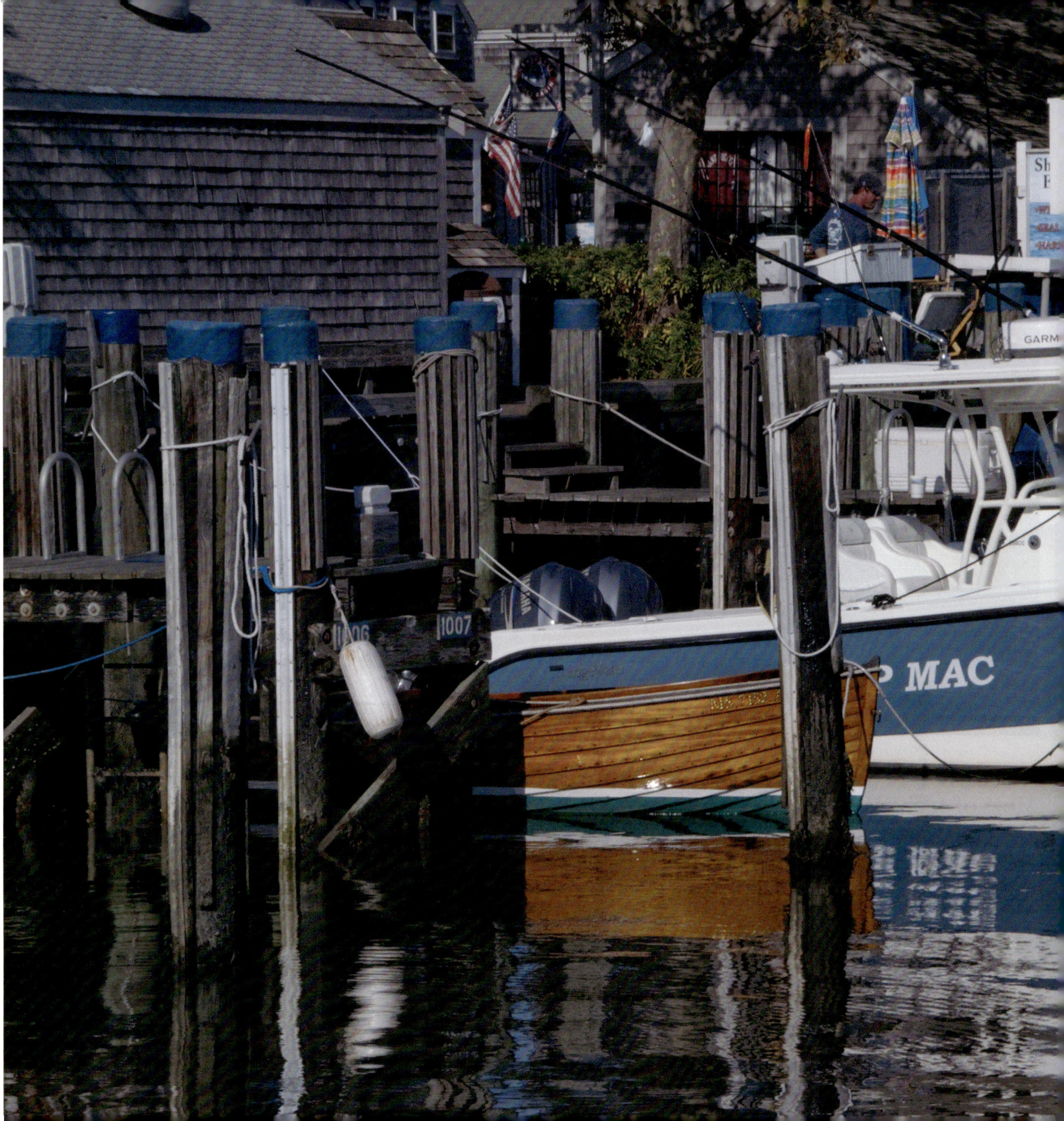
1007
P MAC

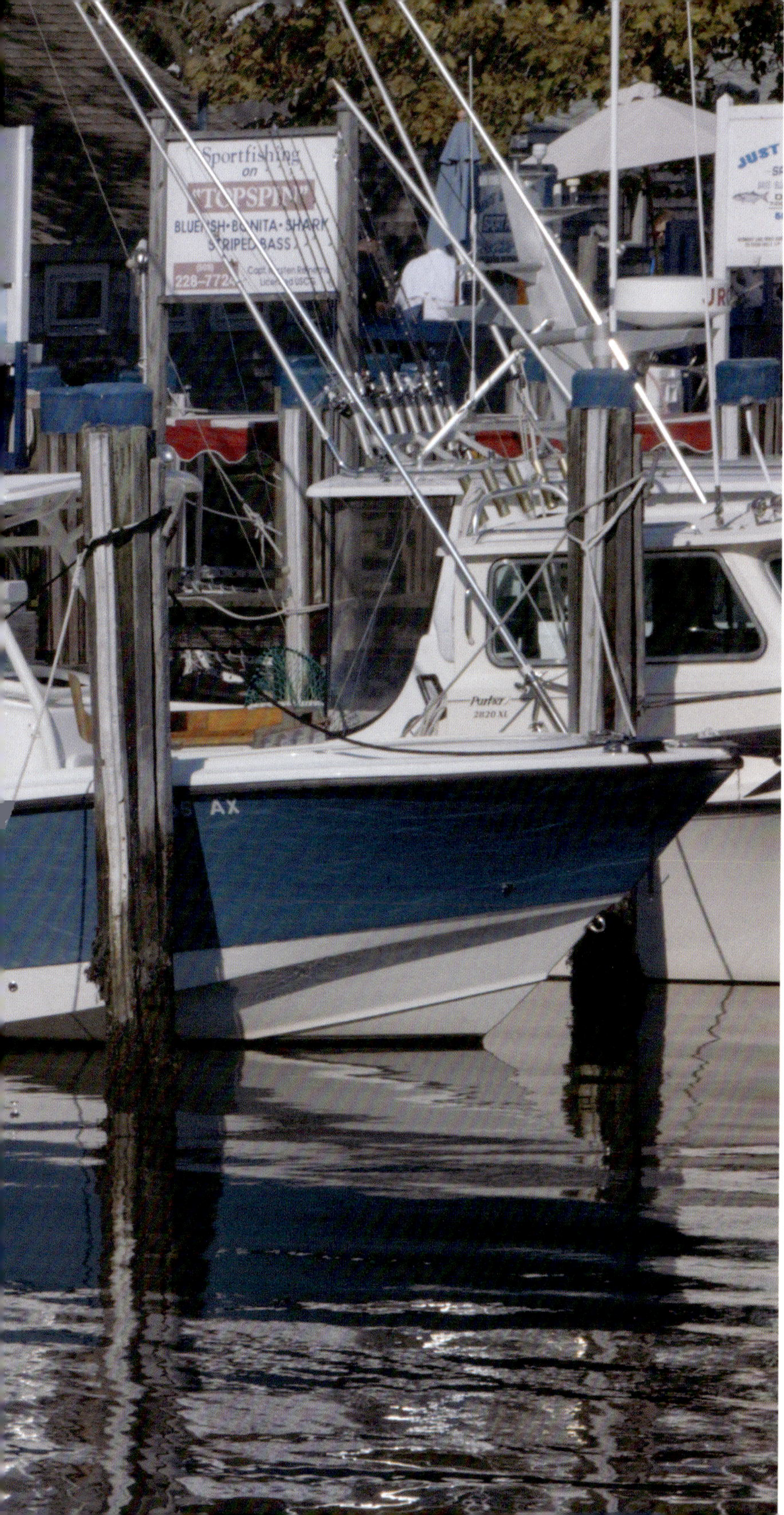

As we travel through this season, we finally have to give up some dreams. We do not win the Nobel Prize, write the great novel, or circumnavigate the globe in a sailboat.

As we approach the end of winter, we are painfully aware with every setting sun that we have seen more in our pasts than we will see in our futures. This is a time of comparing ourselves and our lives with our dreams and expectations.

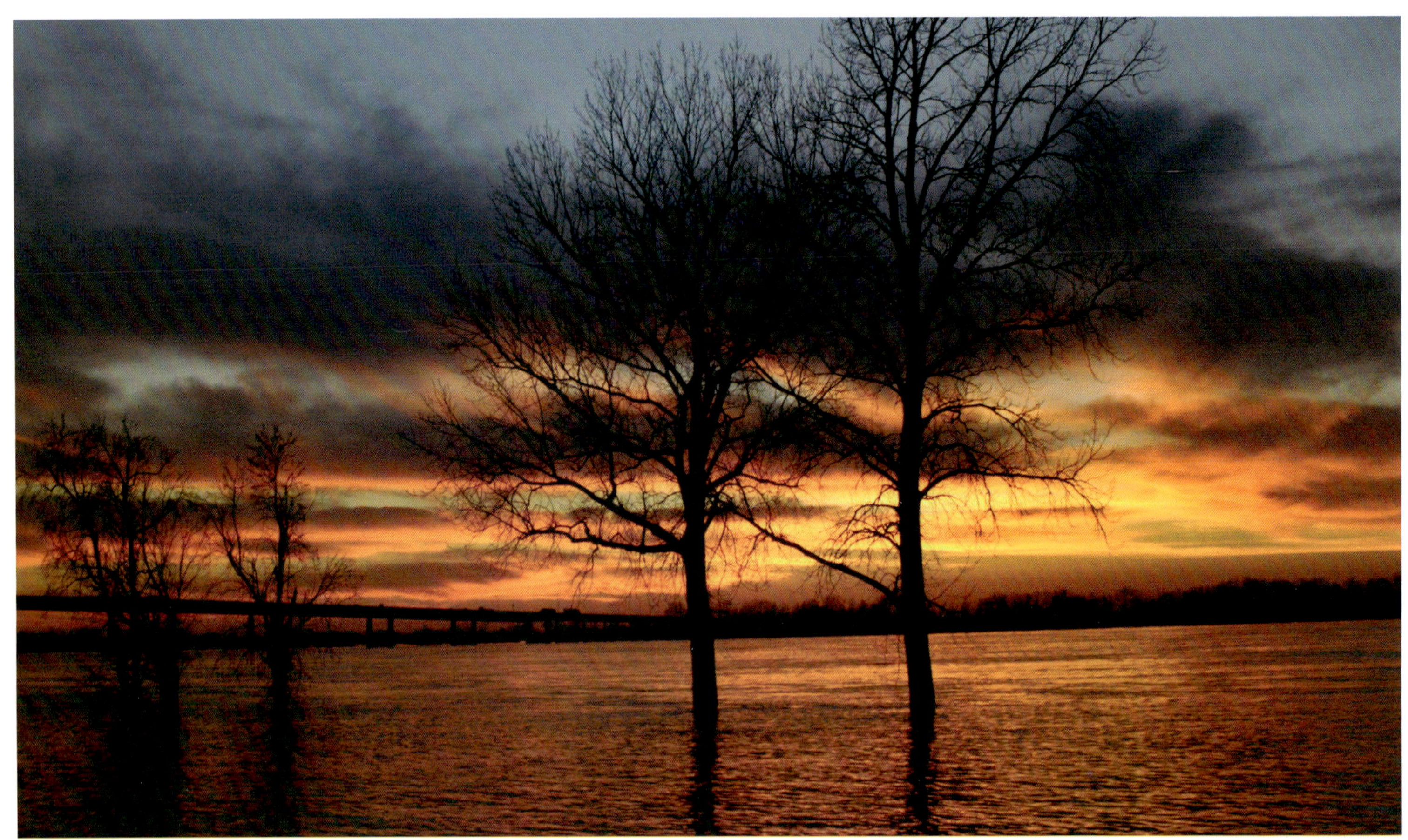

We question whether we are in the right job, the right relationship, the right volunteer spot, the right church, the right body. Have we made some cosmic mistake we can correct on our own?

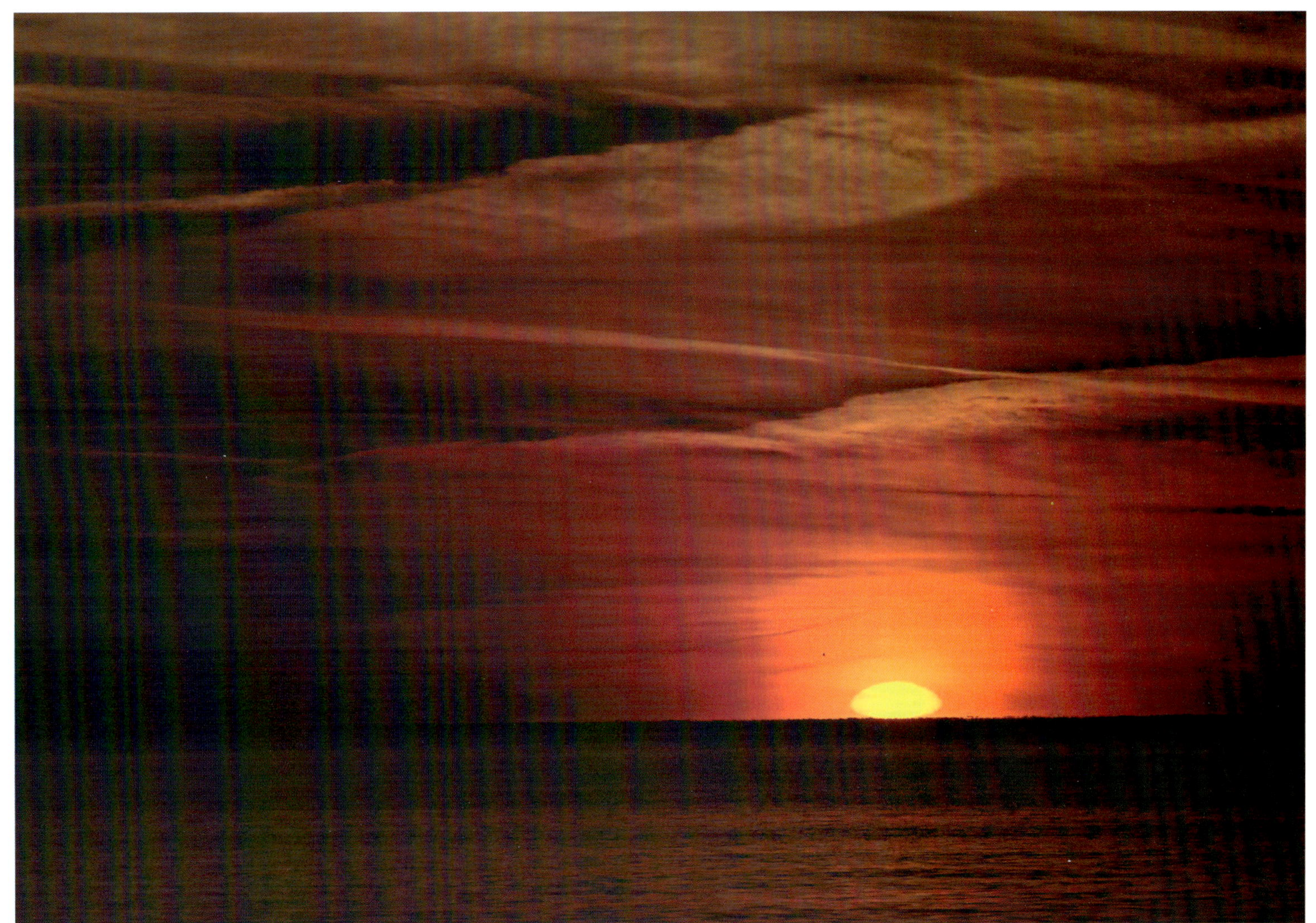

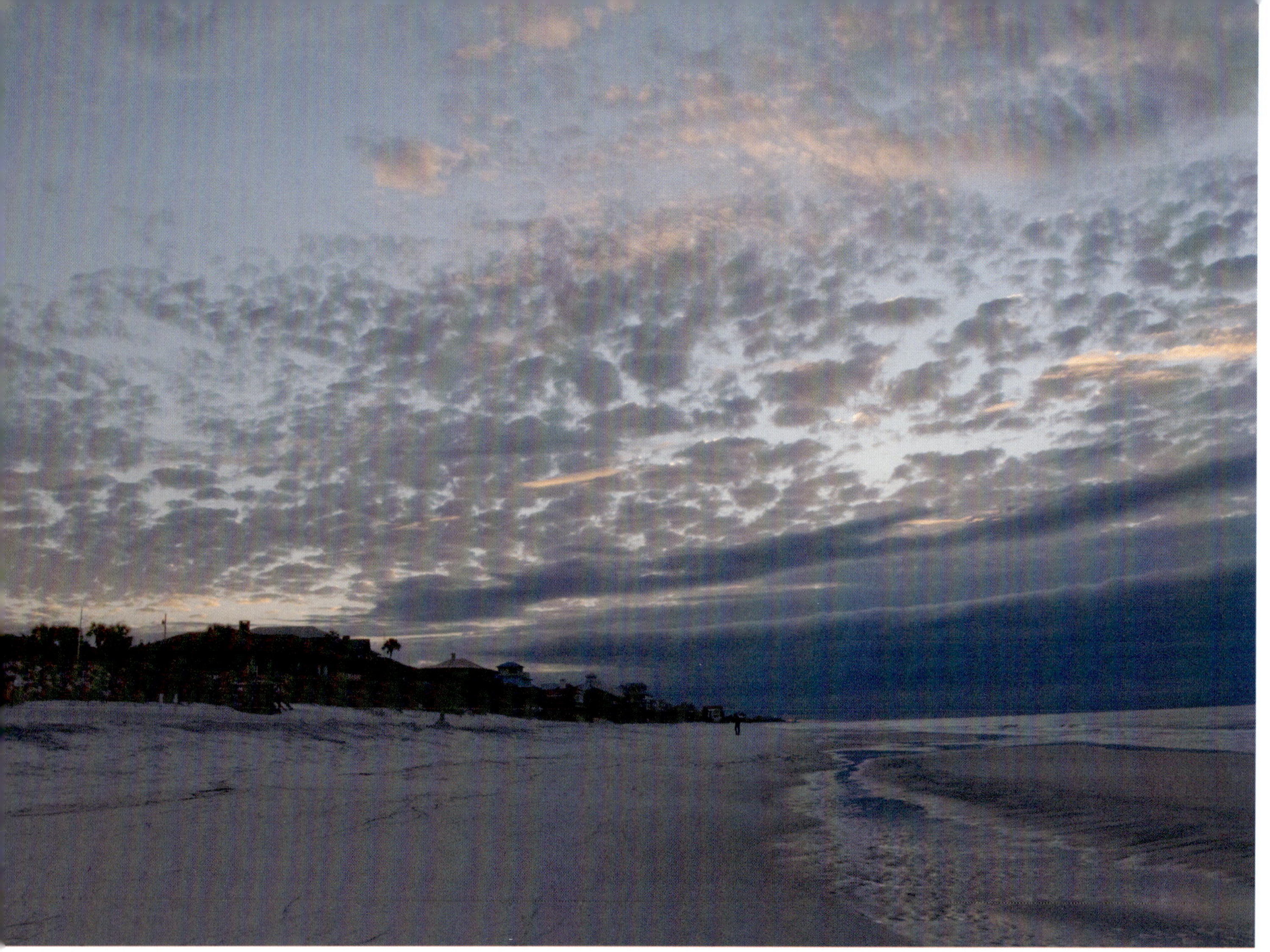

Some of us live alone by the time we reach our fifties, due to death or divorce or never having found the right partner. If we've raised children, when they are finally gone, we may struggle with what to do next. Just getting up in the morning to an empty house can be daunting.

Then there are the health issues. A trainer I knew once told me that because most of us get more sedentary as time goes by, we put on weight even when we haven't changed our eating patterns.

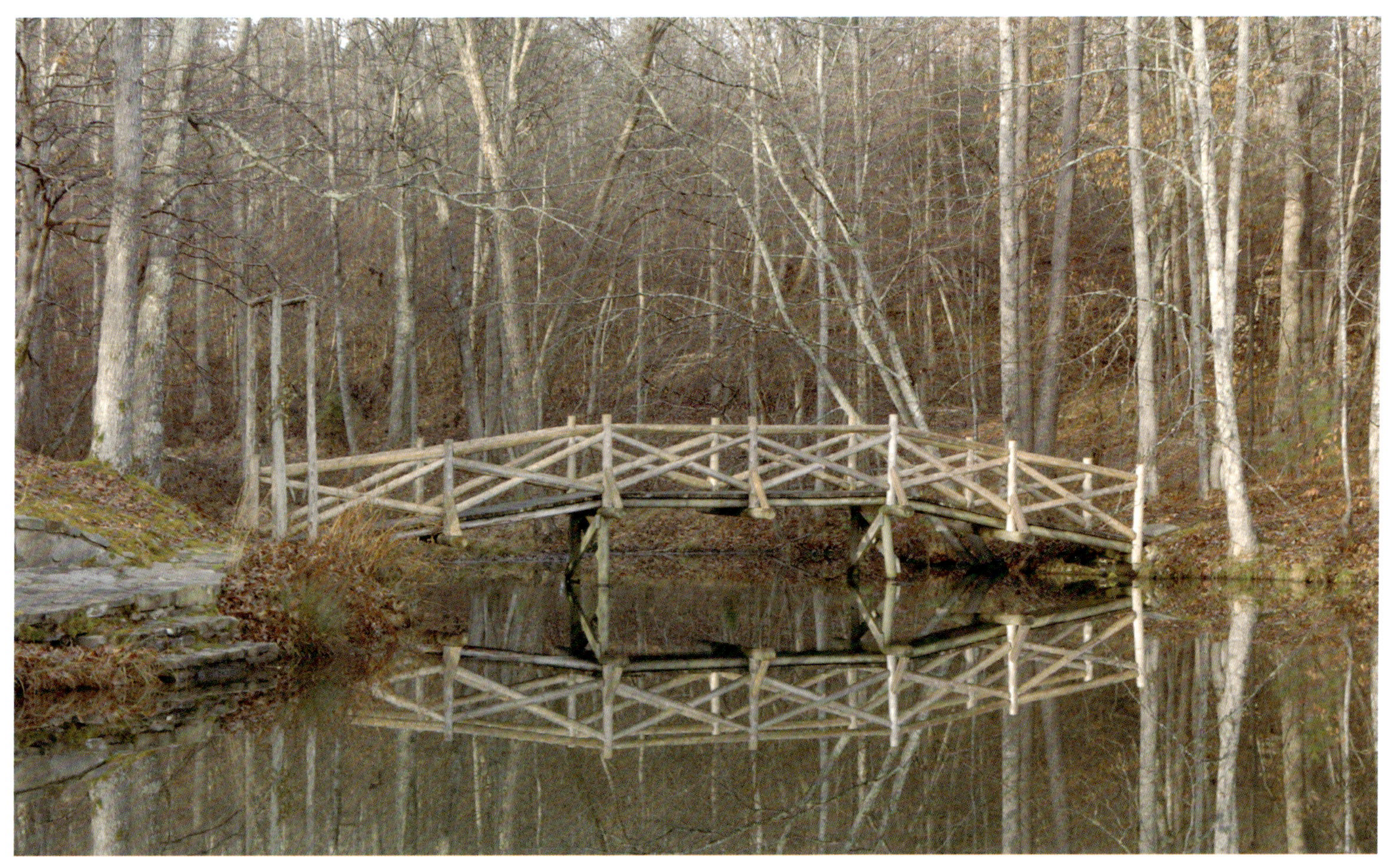

She explained that a pound of muscle burns around sixty calories a day. If, after age forty, we don't exercise regularly, we typically lose a pound of muscle a year. Theoretically, by age fifty, we might lose ten pounds of muscle. This translates into not burning six hundred calories a day that we used to burn.

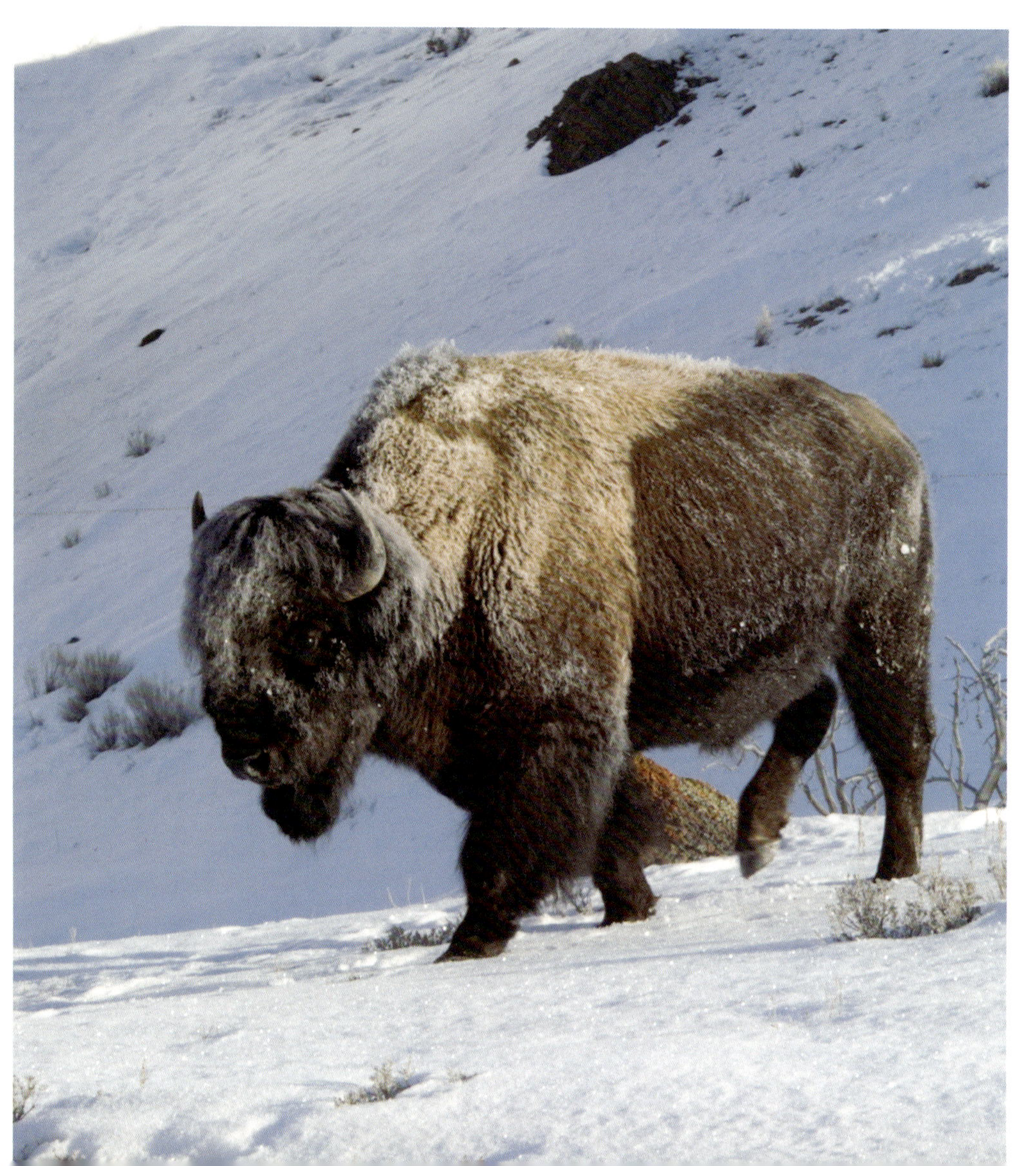

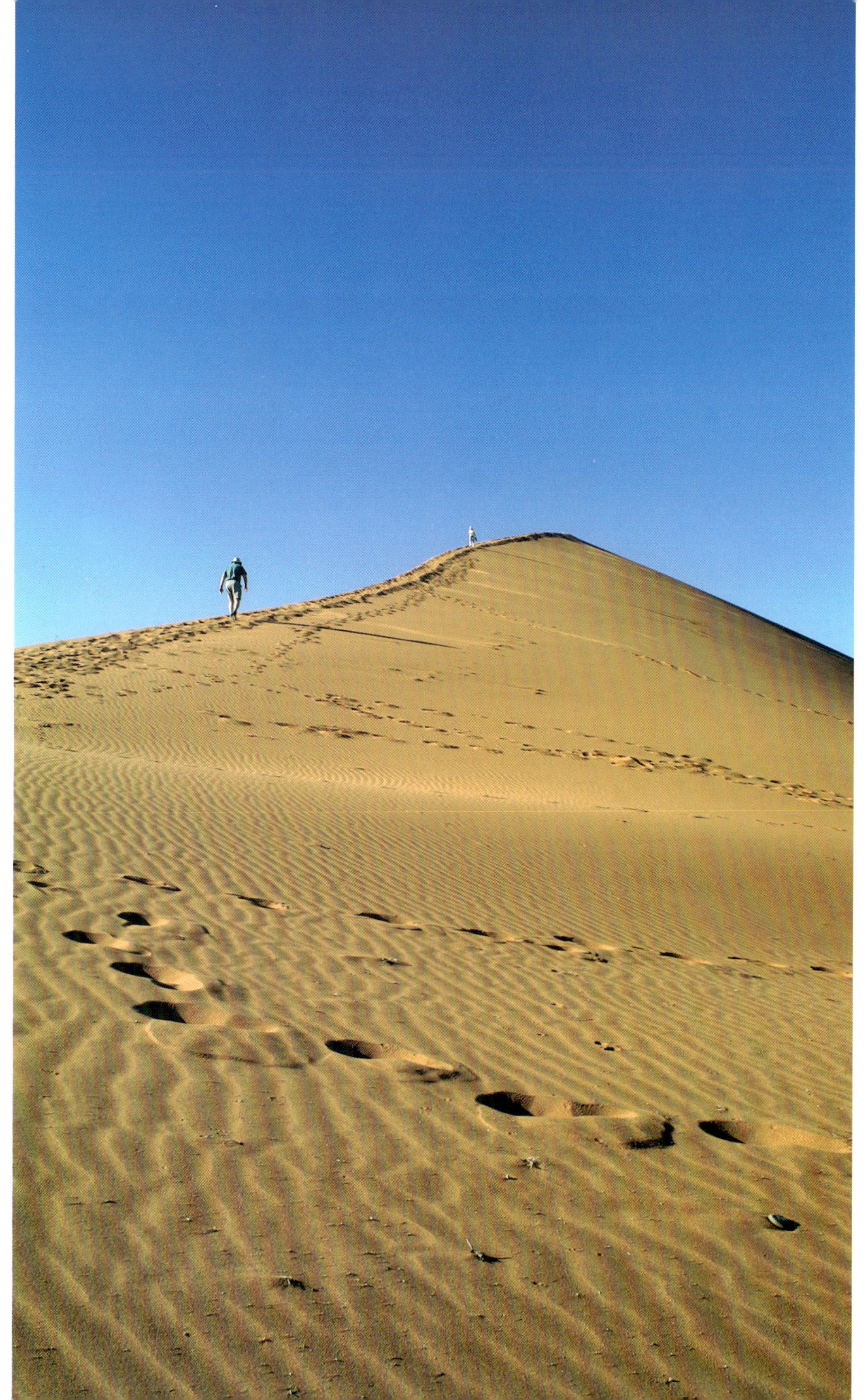

That got my attention. Since our legs have the largest muscle potential, I decided I would run and walk as long as I am physically able in order to delay losing muscle mass. Many face serious physical obstacles at this season, ranging from diabetes to the dreaded "C" word to heart attacks and strokes. The benefit that often comes with these frightening diagnoses is the reality that we still have some control over our lives. How we handle the challenges is our choice.

This is the time to look for guidance and to follow those who have gone before us. Books, magazine articles, support groups, friends, and family who have had similar experiences are all resources that can help us cope.

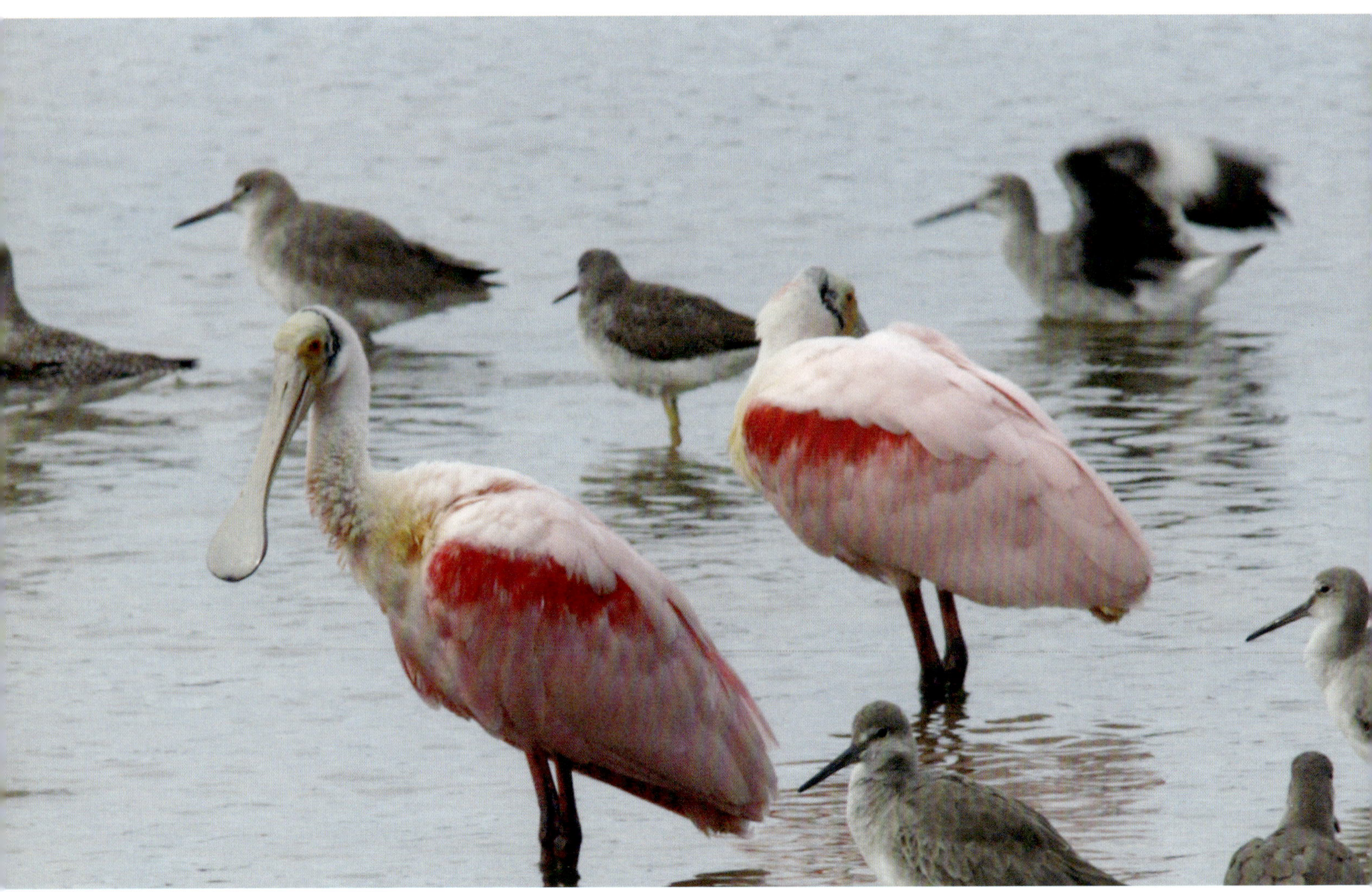

As I ran close to the sixty-year mark, I decided to follow in the footsteps of my father's mother, Johnnie, who never let me call her by anything other than her given name. She wore bright colors and was flamboyant. Like a bird of gorgeous plumage, she stood out in a crowd. Well, why not?

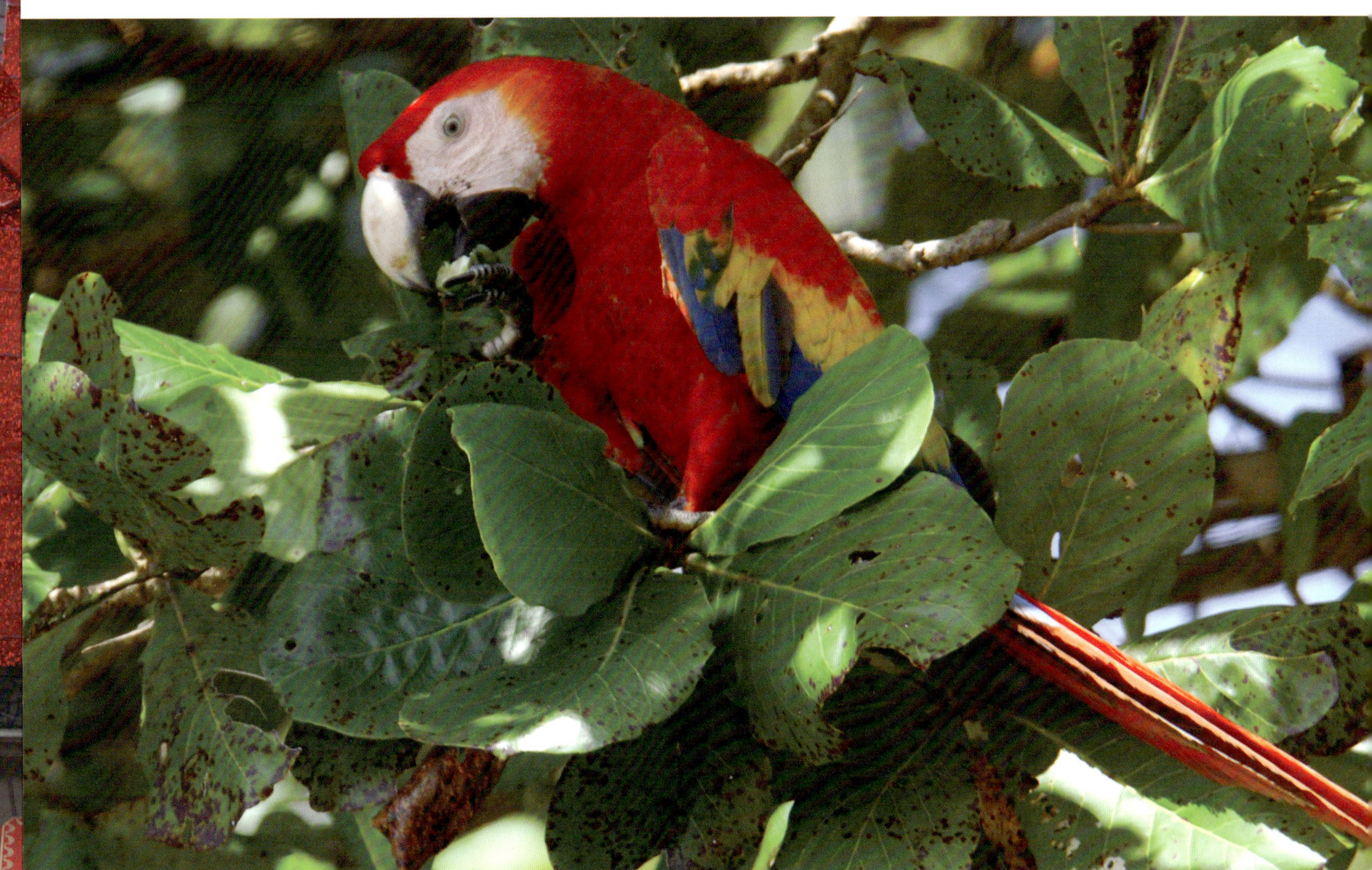

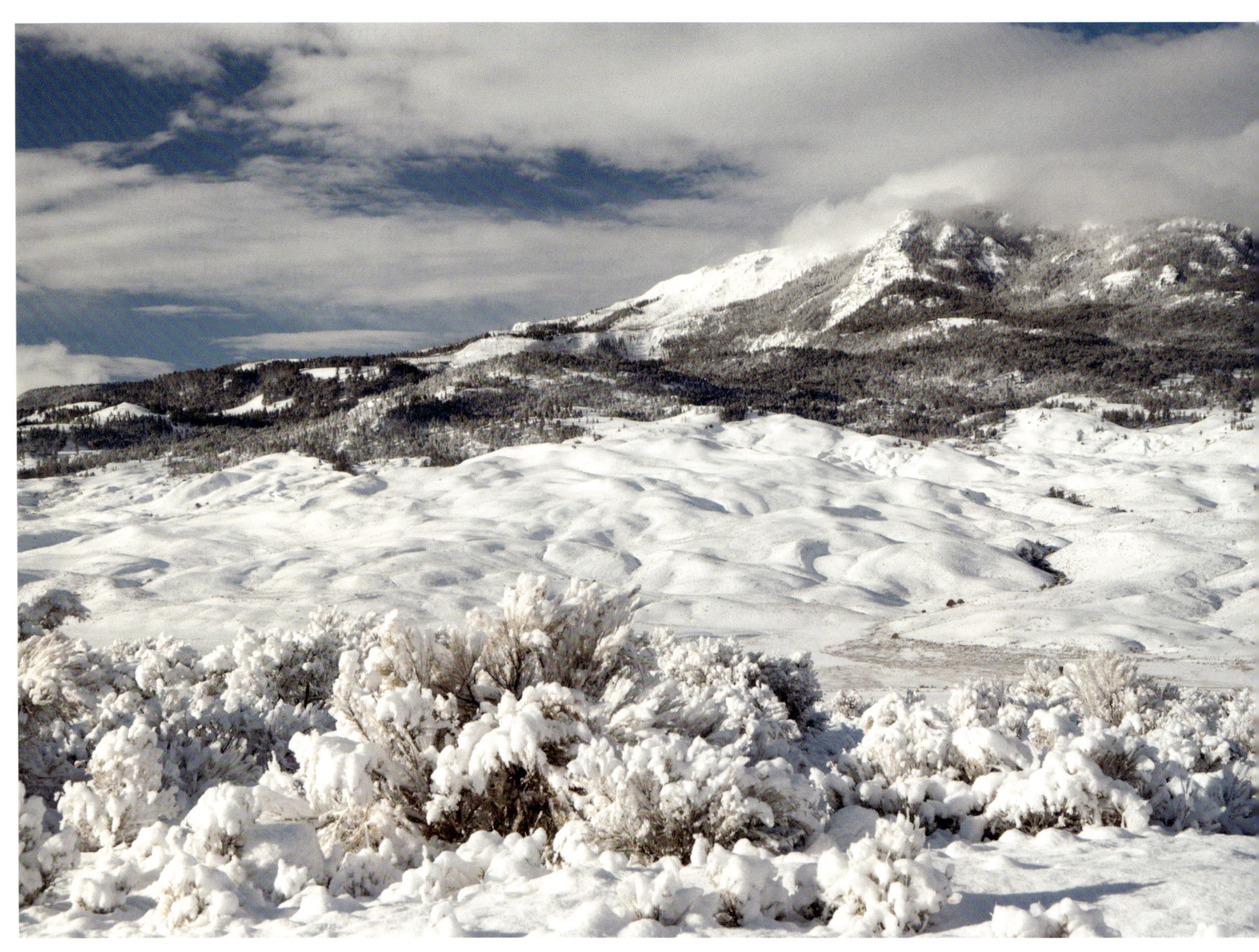

7

Lesson Learned in Winter

Celebrate Differences

When do we first take note that some people are different from us or, alternatively, that we are quite different from most others? We might have had mixed feelings, but probably we experienced a sense of pride when we were told we were like our mother or father or an older sibling. Hearing this strengthened our sense of place, of belonging.

Subconsciously, if not consciously, hearing a parent or other relative criticize someone and comment that "They aren't like us" may have been the first moment we became aware that perhaps we aren't all alike. Later, we probably established a subliminal hierarchy, noting who was "better" and who was "worse" than we were.

If we were fortunate enough to go to school with children of different ethnic, cultural, and socio-economic backgrounds and actually developed friendships with these "others," we learned valuable lessons. We, all of us, in this richly diverse United States of America, are much more alike as individuals and as families than we are different.

If, when growing up, we associated only with people exactly like ourselves, we were underprivileged. Today, even rural areas are ethnically diverse. The earlier we learn to appreciate and celebrate our differences, the easier it is to adjust to new situations, whether it's going off to college and having a Pakistani roommate or getting our first job and being the only Latino in the room.

We are all products of a loving Creator. We don't pick our parents, so we can't take credit or rightfully we feel entitled for having been born into supportive families in good neighborhoods. Look at the strength we see in family ties in every neighborhood. We each need to learn as much as we can about the positive aspects of other approaches to life. We can enrich our own lives by opening our hearts and minds and adapting what we learn.

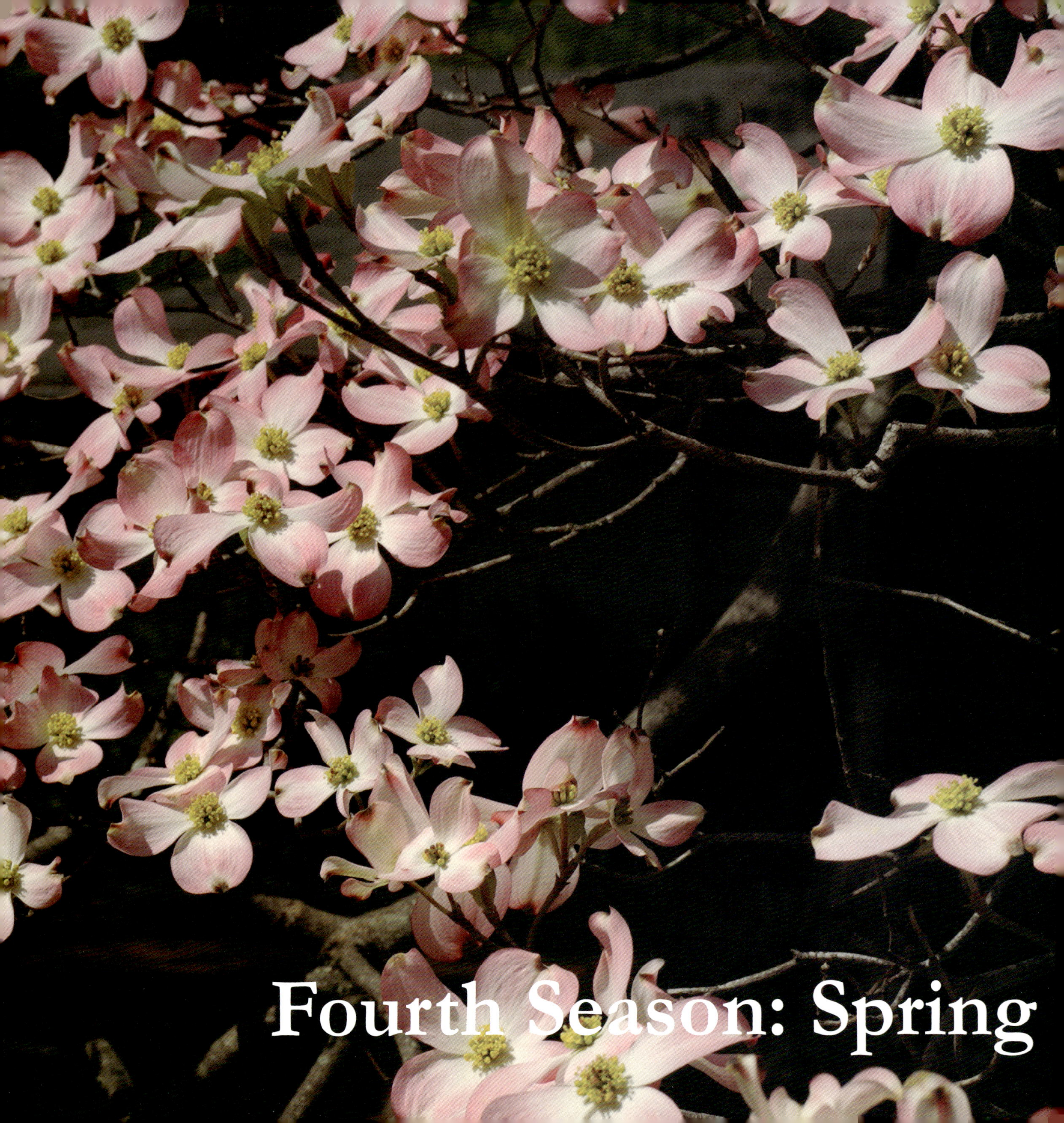

Fourth Season: Spring

Why I Wake Early

by Mary Oliver

Hello, sun in my face.
Hello, you who make the morning
and spread it over the fields
and into the faces of the tulips
and the nodding morning glories,
and into the windows of, even, the
miserable and the crotchety –

best preacher that ever was,
dear star, that just happens
to be where you are in the universe
to keep us from ever-darkness,
to ease us with warm touching,
to hold us in the great hands of light –
good morning, good morning, good morning.

Watch, now, how I start the day
in happiness, in kindness.

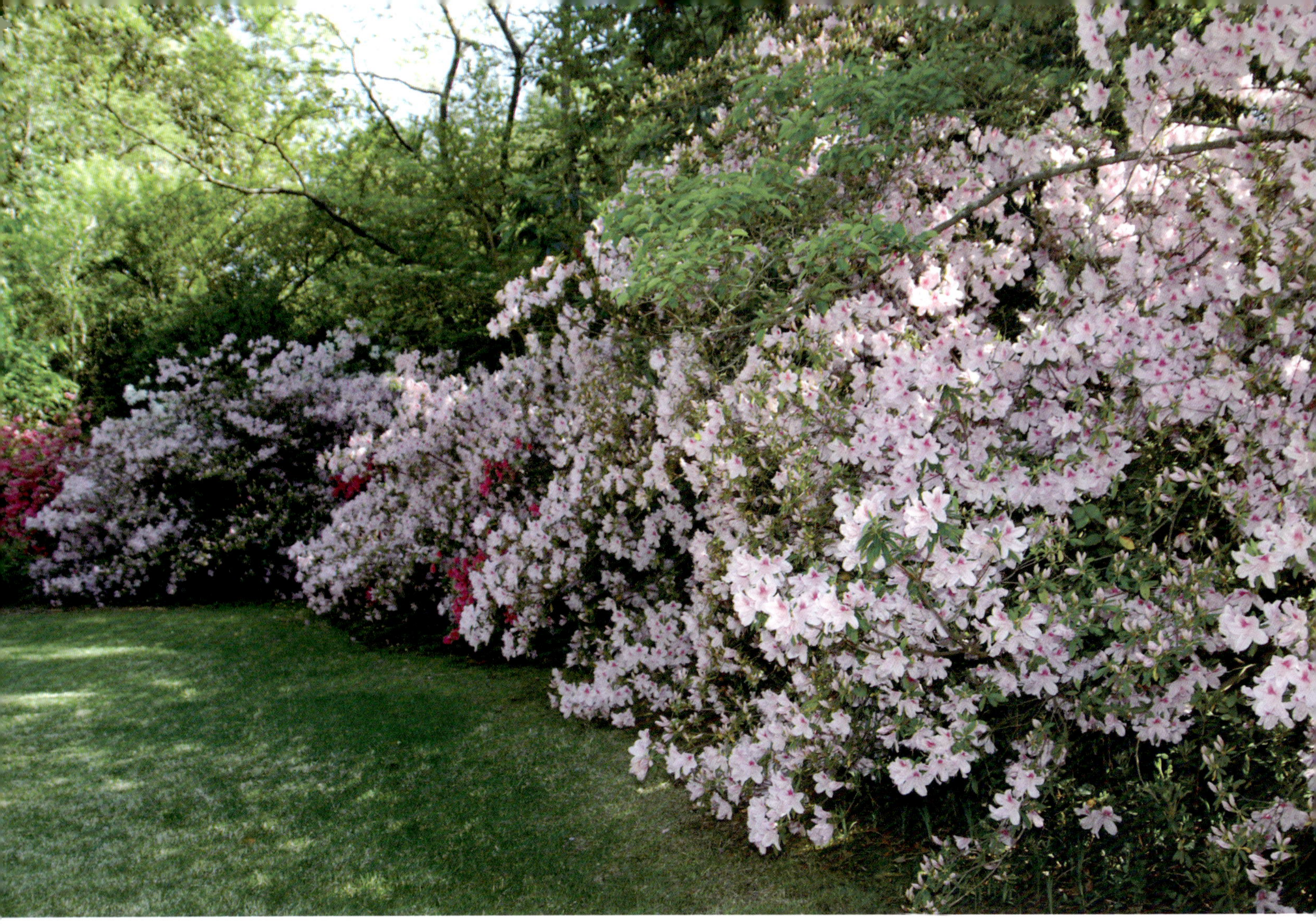

Spring is the season with the best press. It symbolizes birth, newness, freshness, and beauty. The surprise of a long life may well be the realization that this is the best season after all.

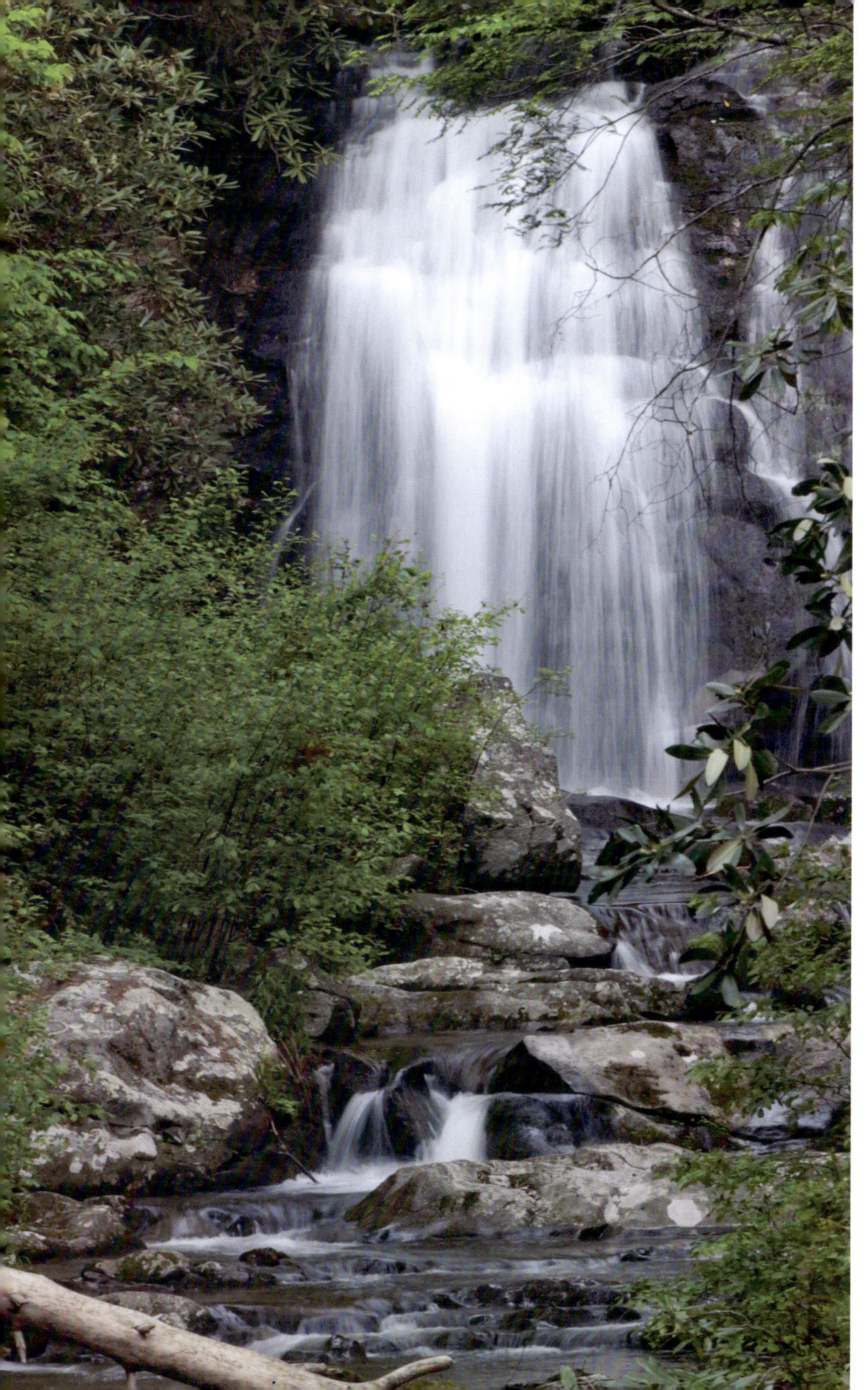

As the famous "Baby Boomers" turn sixty, it is apparent that they are wealthier as a group than their predecessors. Apart from those who have become obese, they are also healthier. Are they also happier, or can they be?

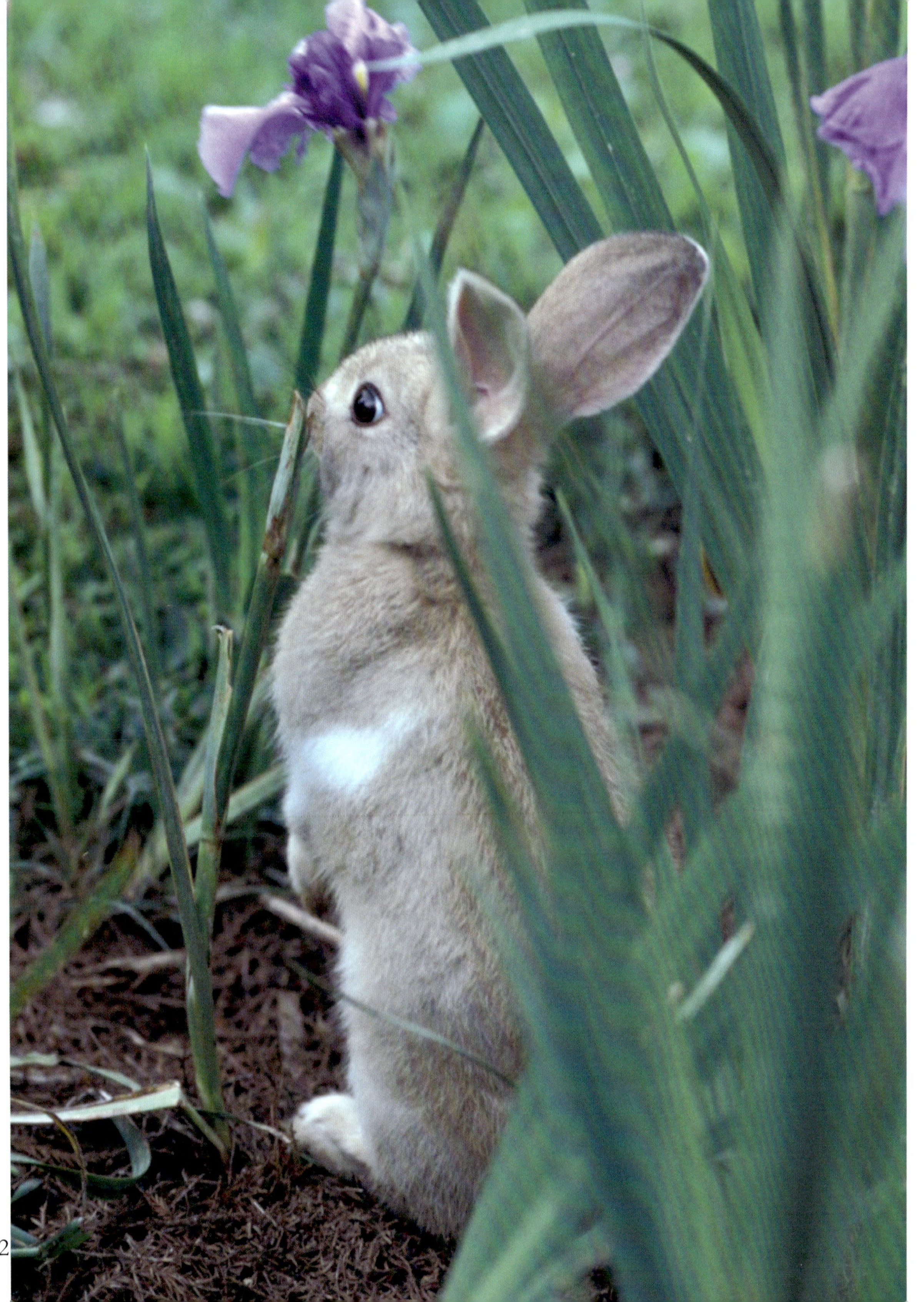

People ages sixty and up are on the front lines, standing between their children and the brink of eternity. The advantage of so many birthdays to look back on gives us an automatic cachet of knowledge achieved simply by breathing longer than our deceased friends and family members. Our variety and abundance of experiences help balance our thought processes and attitudes.

Our families of worship, found both inside and outside the walls of organized congregations, become more important to us as we begin the last part of our individual journeys. We look for significance, not just success.

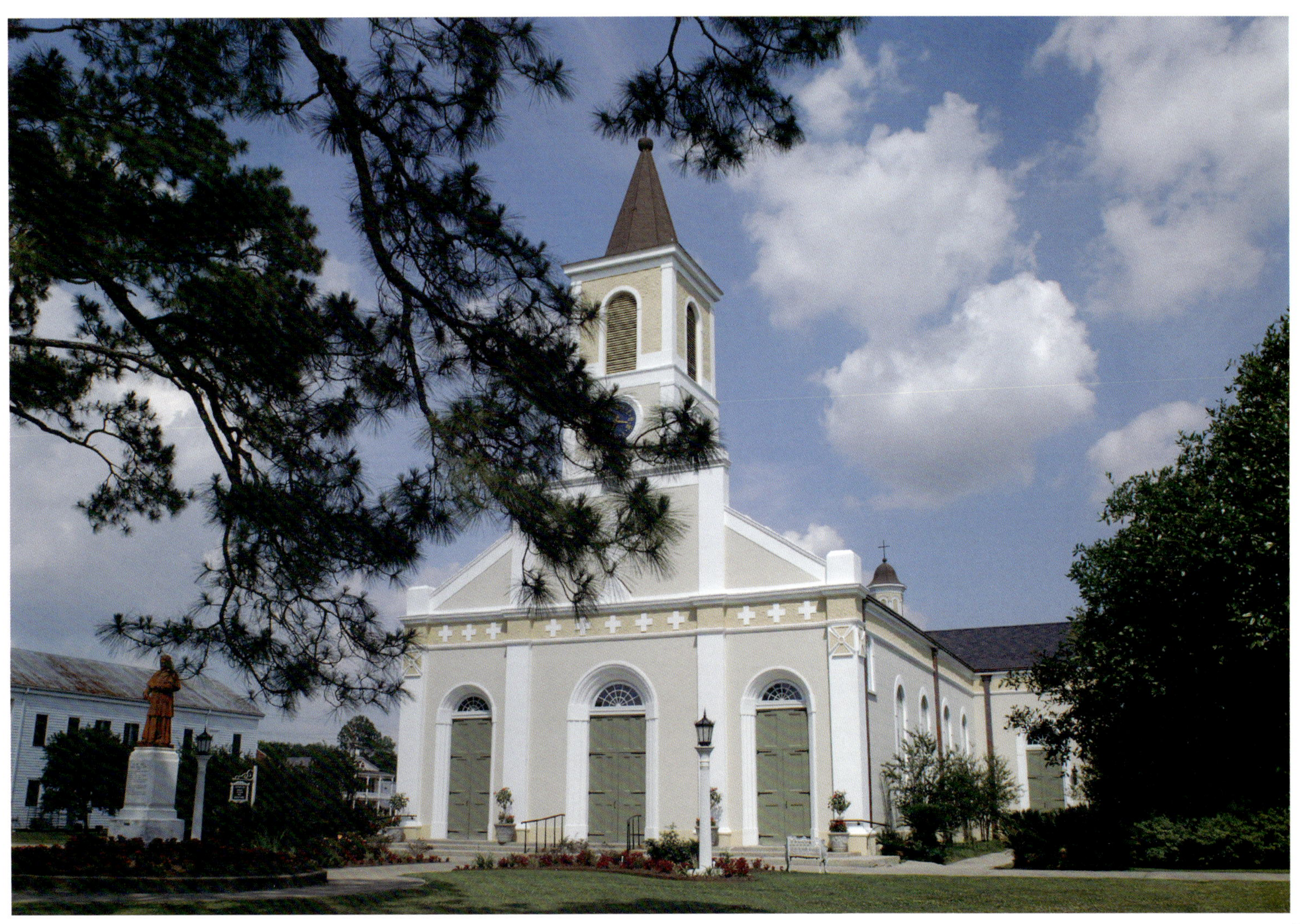

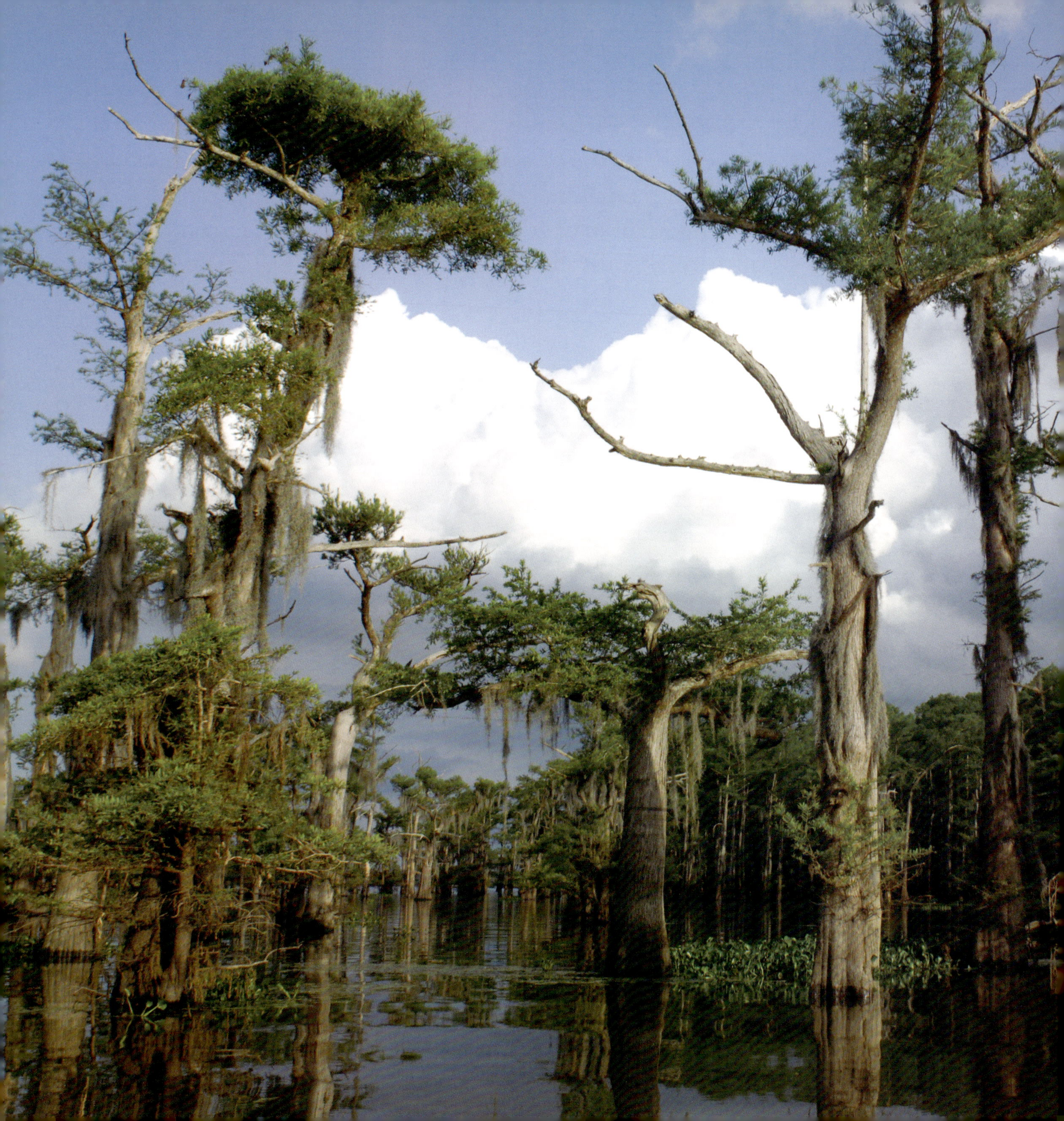

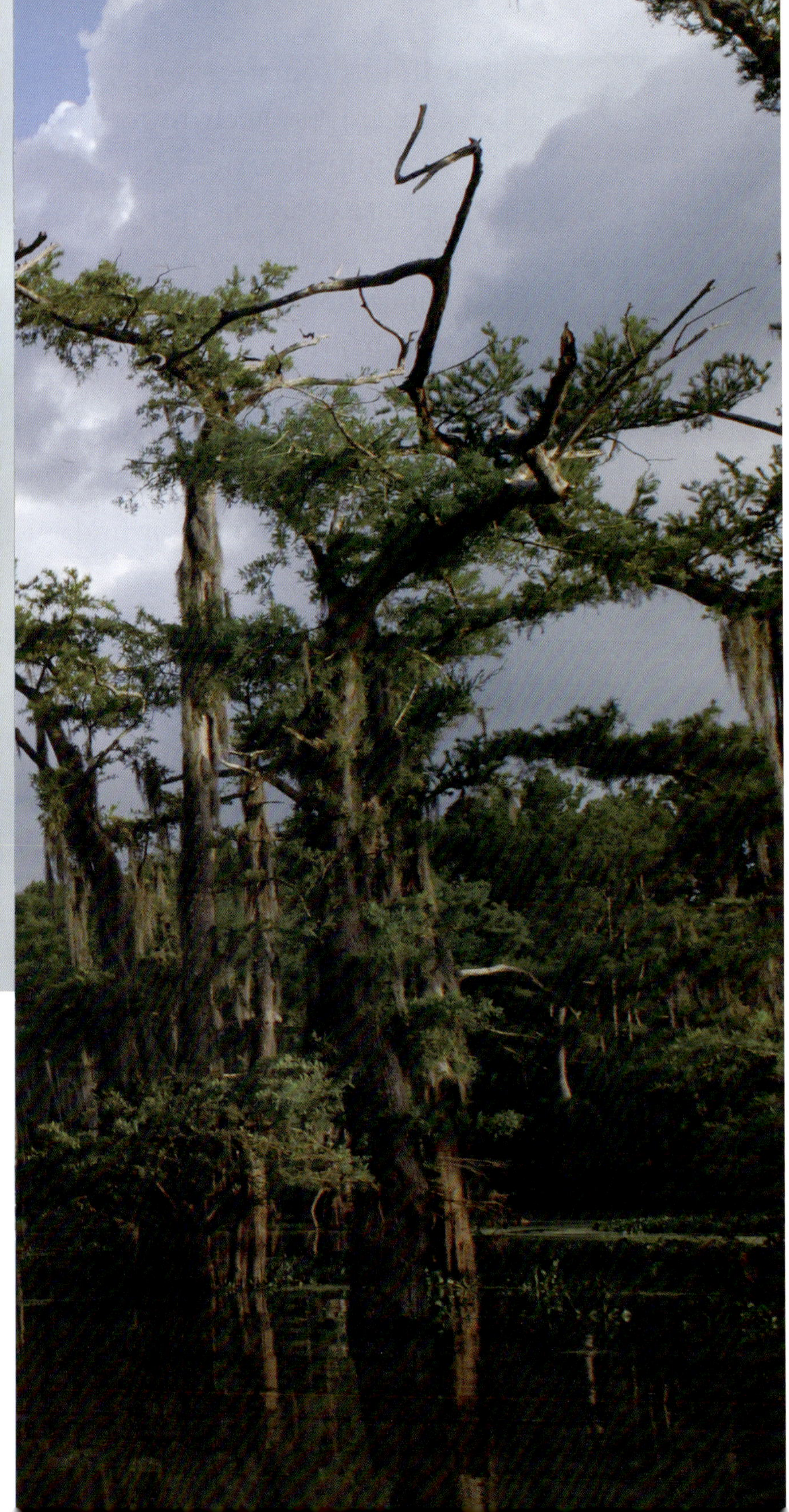

We assimilate multitudinous experiences vicariously from the media, books, and stories others tell us of their lives. Most of these we're not even aware we've absorbed. Synthesized in our brains, they form a foundation that helps us solve the questions we come up against throughout life.

I am reminded of Jenny Joseph's popular poem entitled "Warning: When I Am an Old Woman I Shall Wear Purple." In it, she talks about doing the unexpected, like wearing an unsuitable red hat. Then she opines that she should start practicing wearing purple so people won't be too shocked when she really does get old.

It makes me wonder why indeed we are saving purple and the good china and silver.

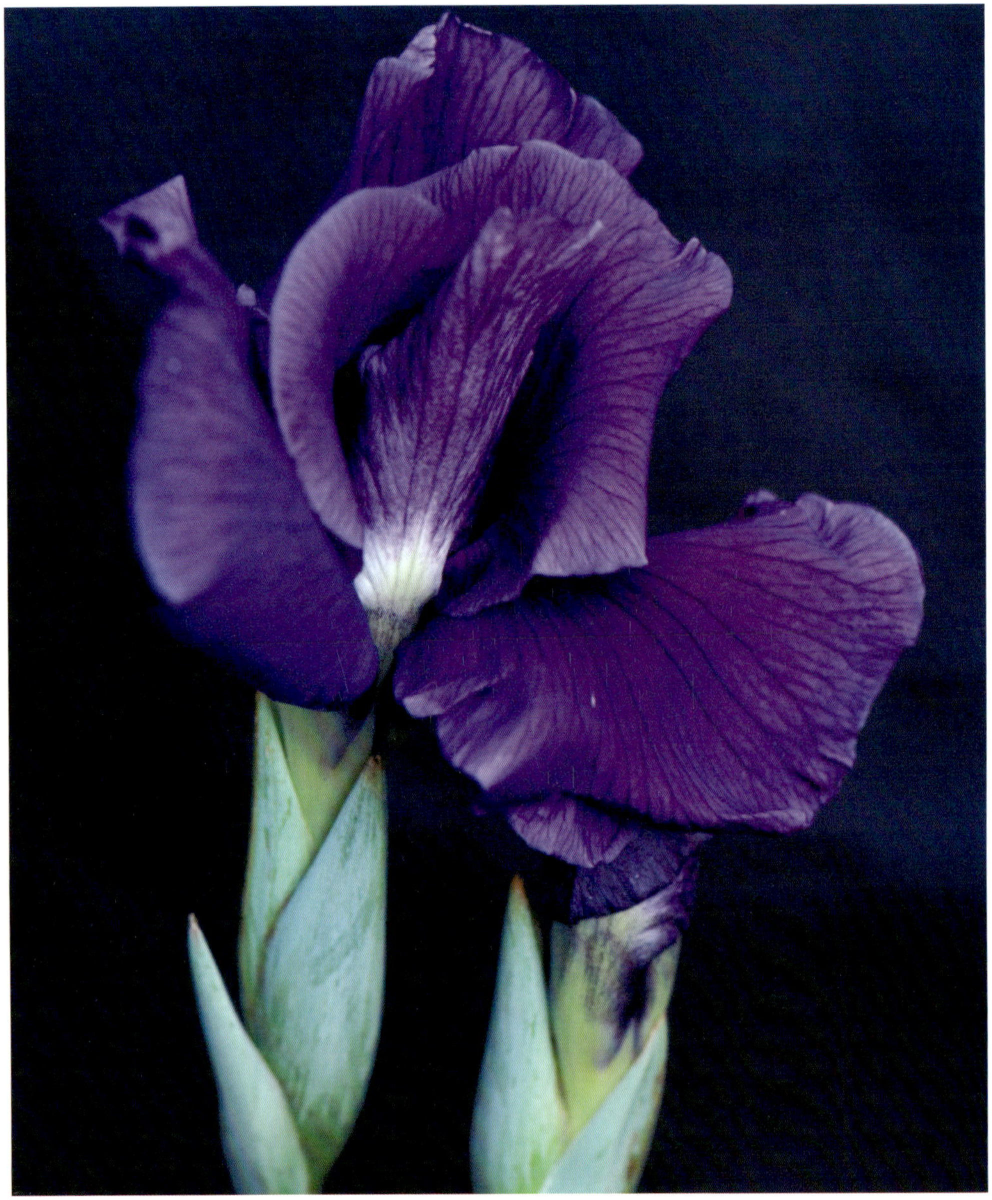

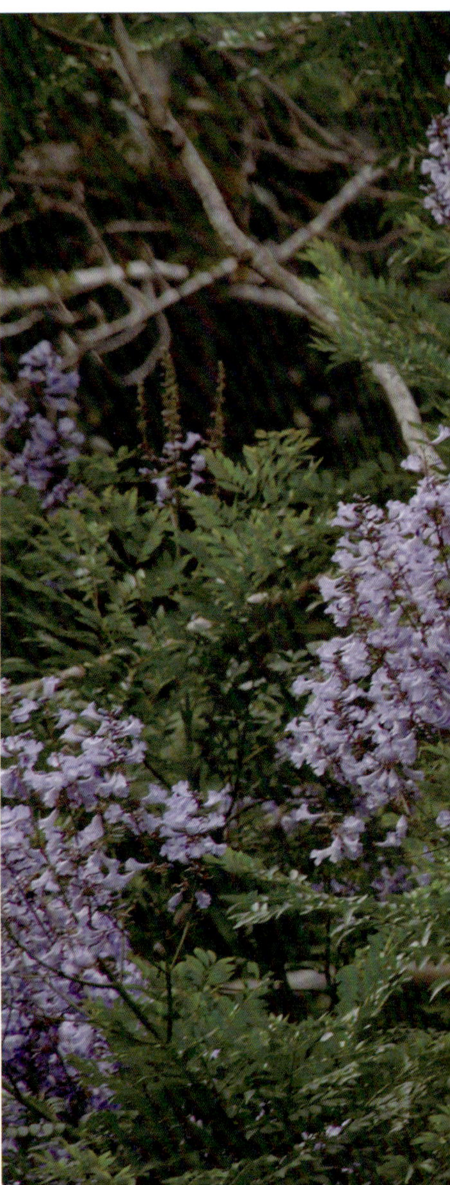

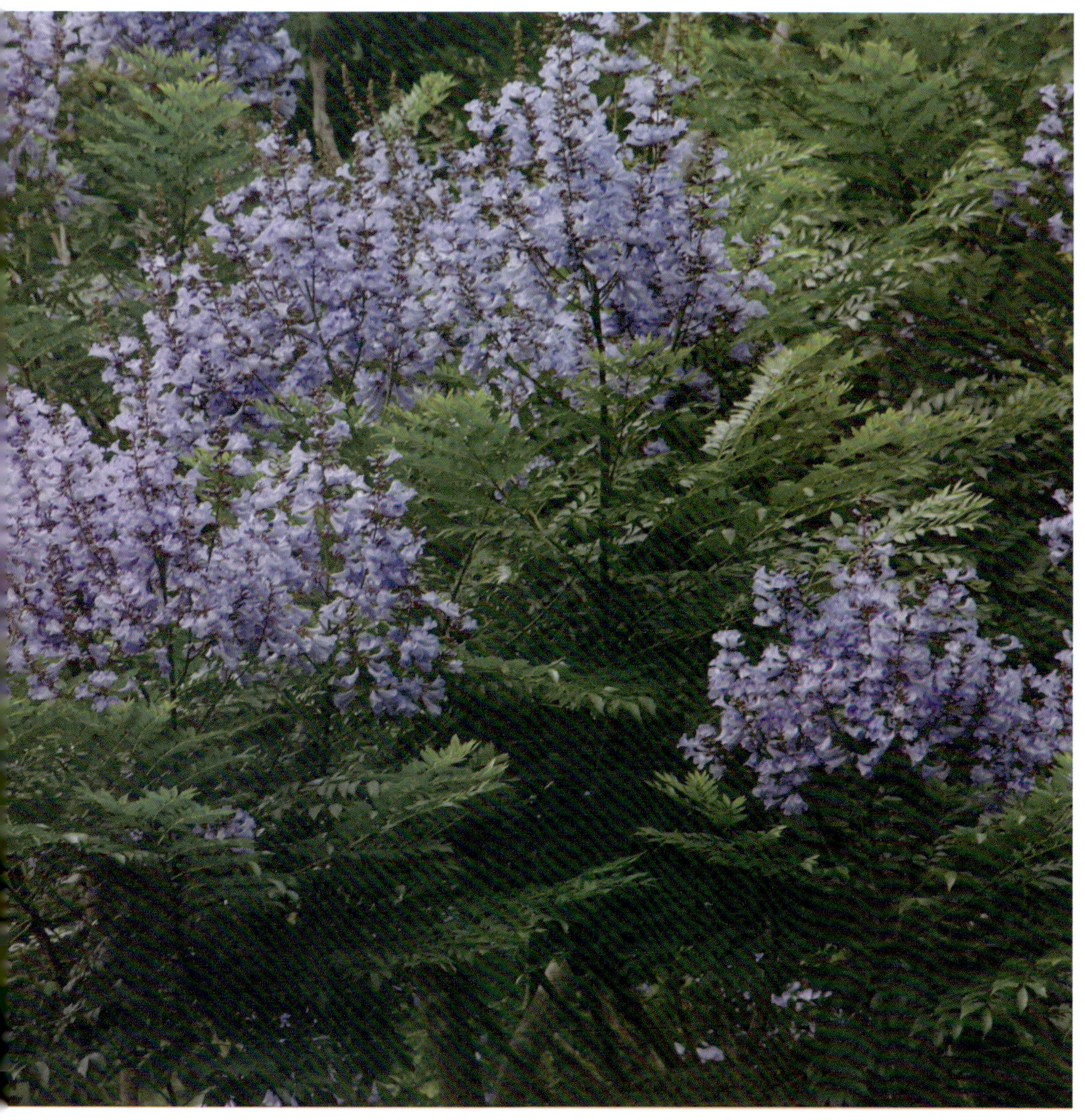

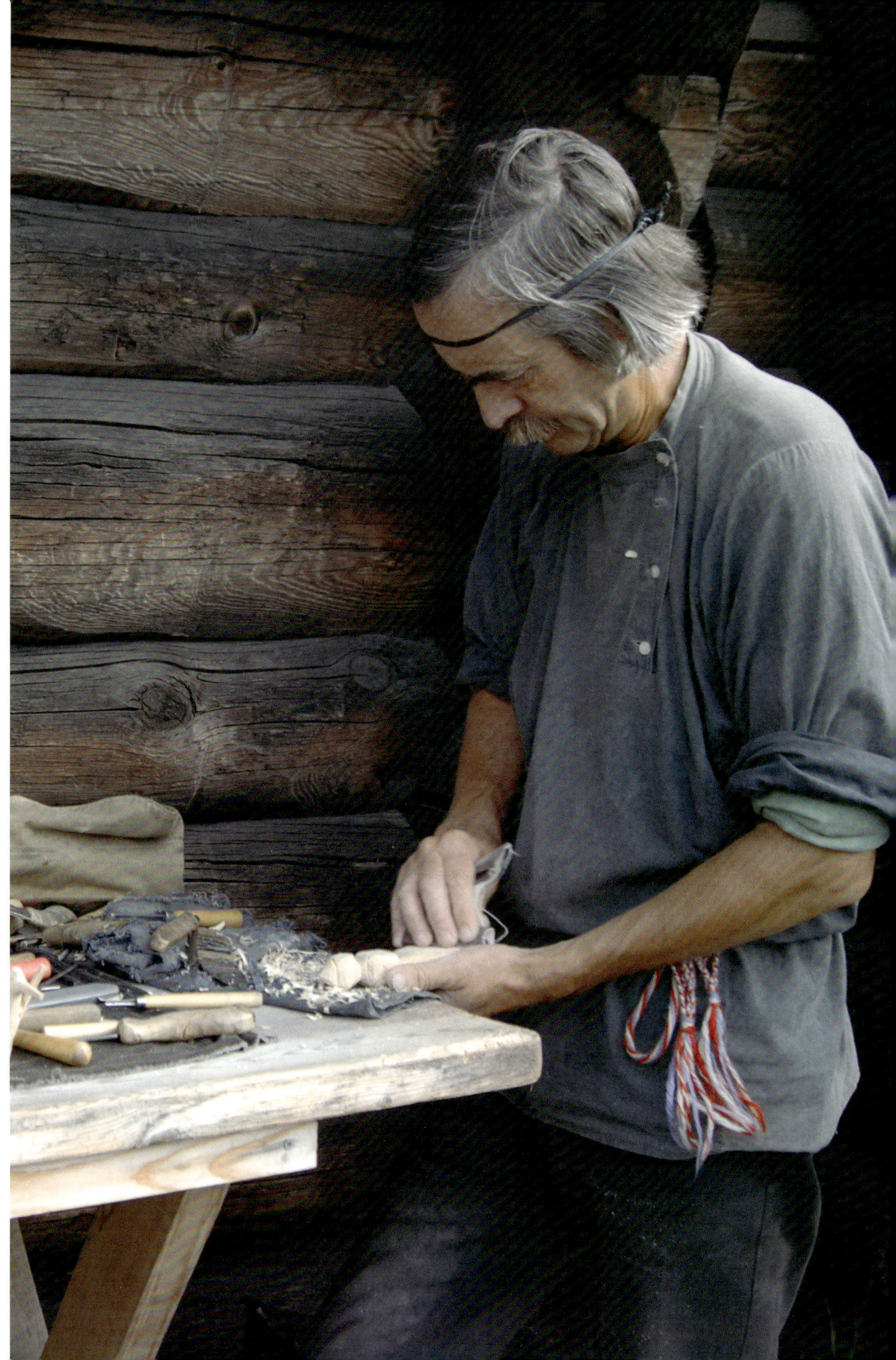

According to U.S. Census estimates, 2017 will mark the first time those who are sixty-five or older will outnumber those under age five. By 2025, ten percent of our total population will be older than sixty-five.

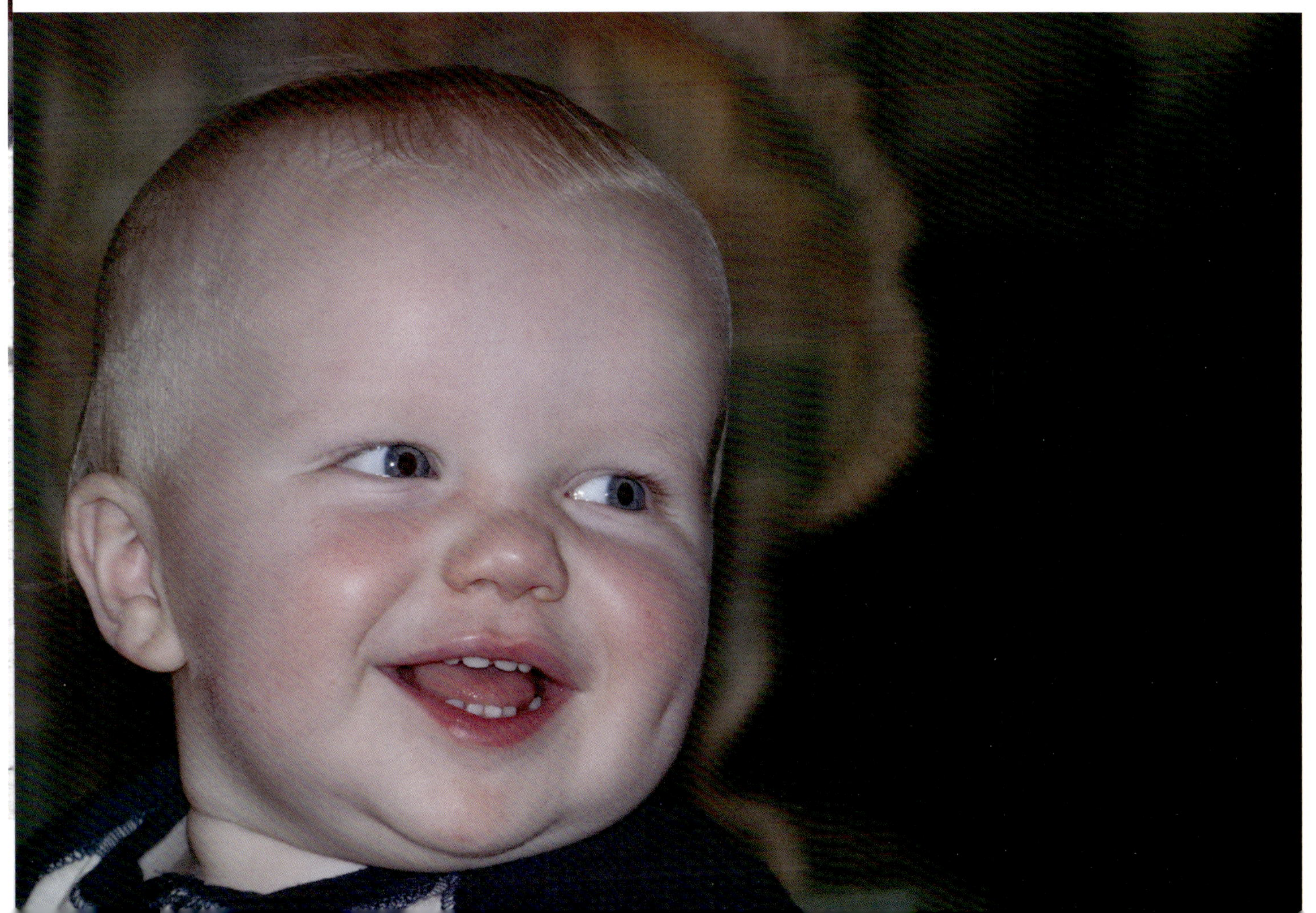

The full consequences of so many of us living longer, healthier lives remain to be seen, but it is reasonable to assume that recognizing the abundance of intellectual capital represented by those in this season of spring could make a significant contribution to improving life for our country as a whole.

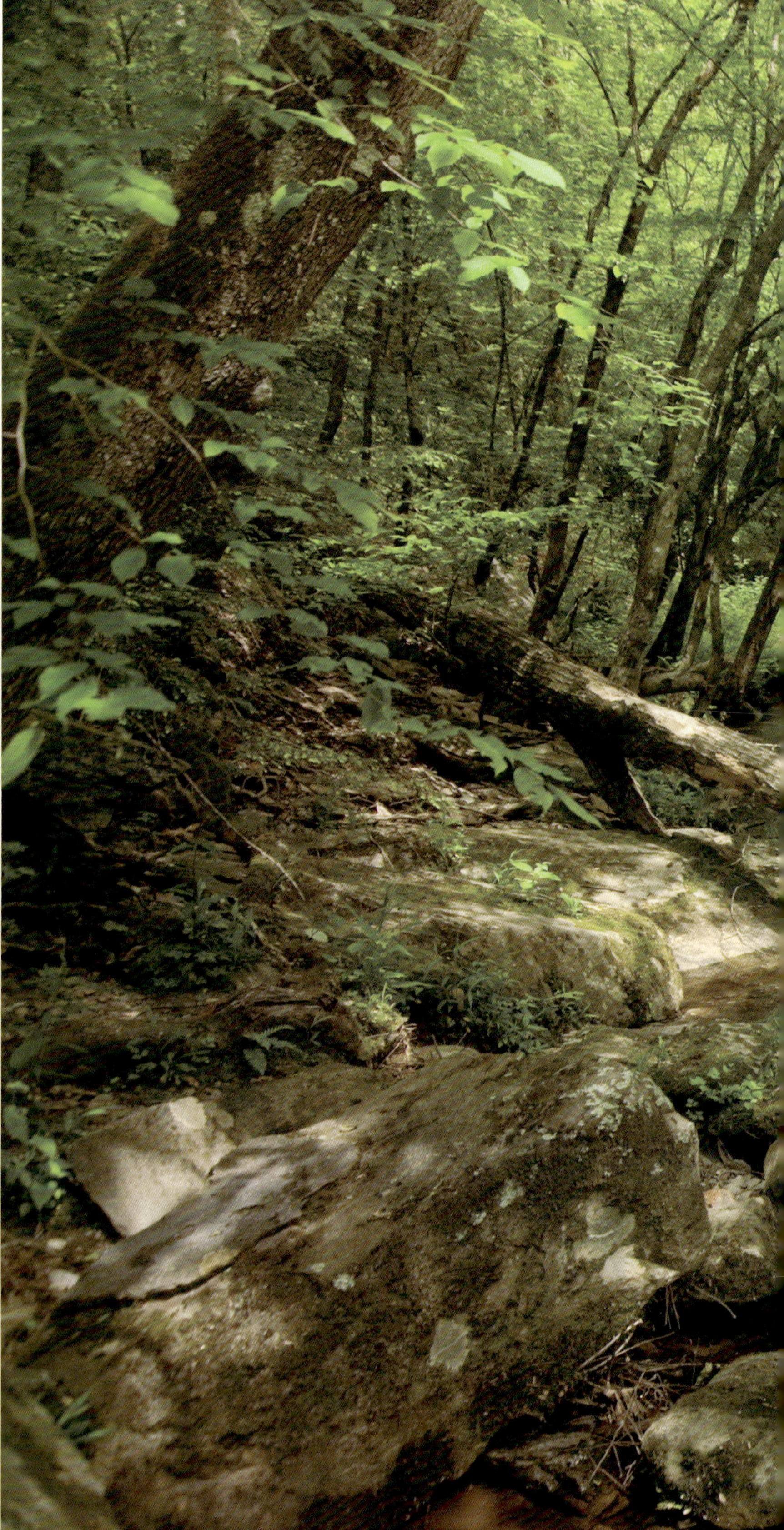

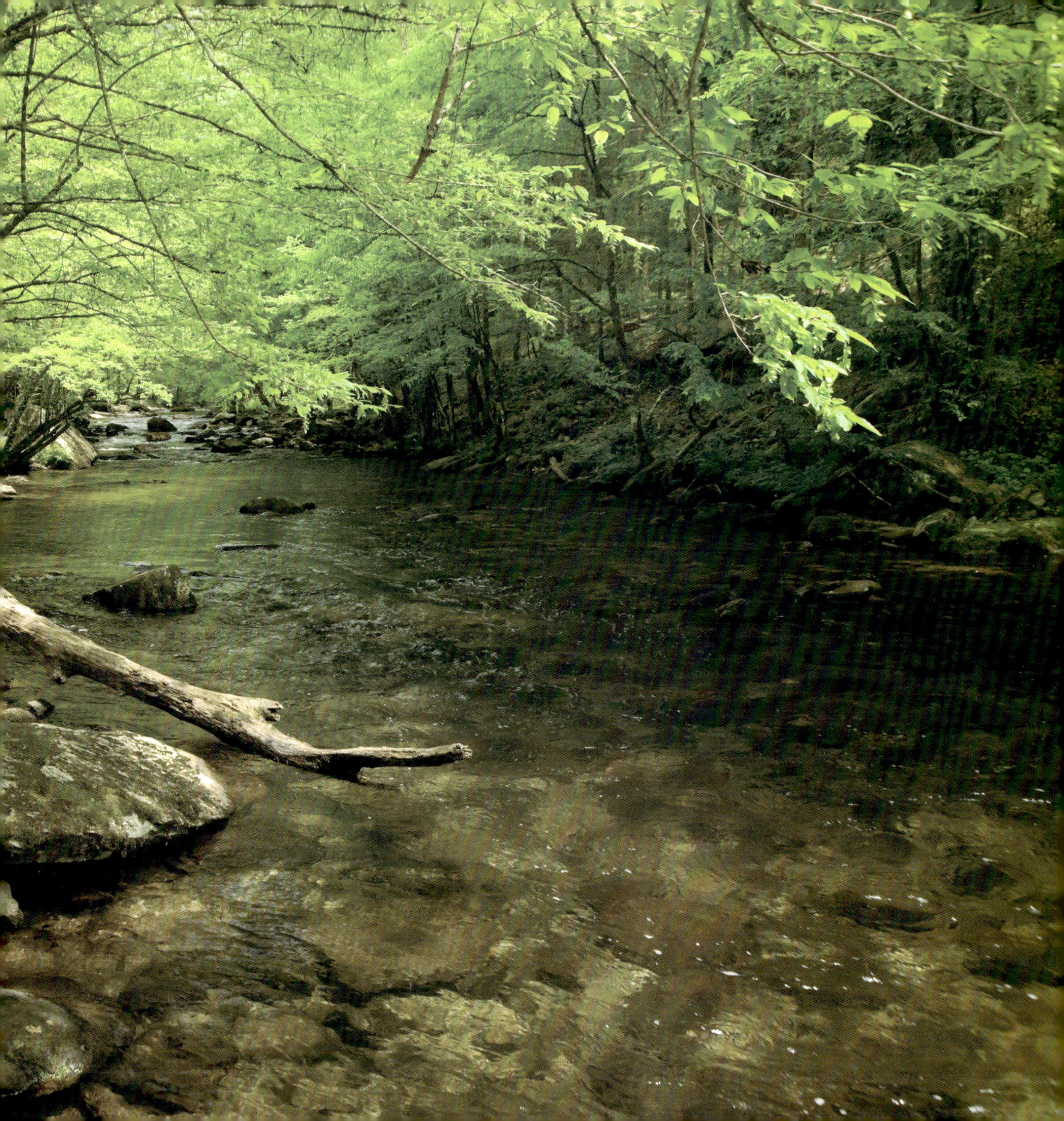

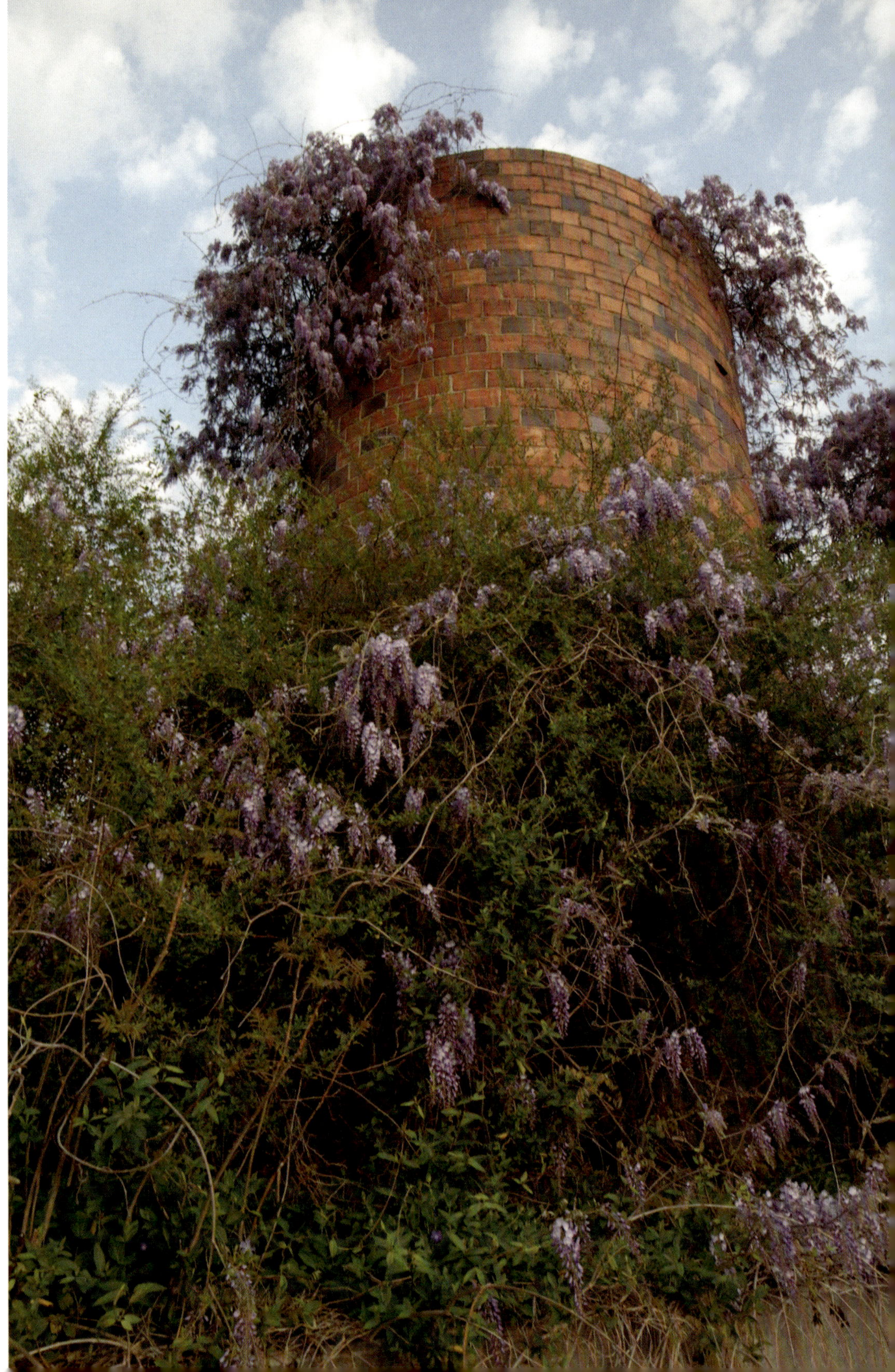

It doesn't take as much imagination as it does organization to create opportunities for those in the springtime of life to be able to share their knowledge and experience with their communities.

Meanwhile, U.S. Census Bureau data shows that in 2008, our country had over three million single-parent households. That year alone, over forty percent of all live births were to unmarried women.

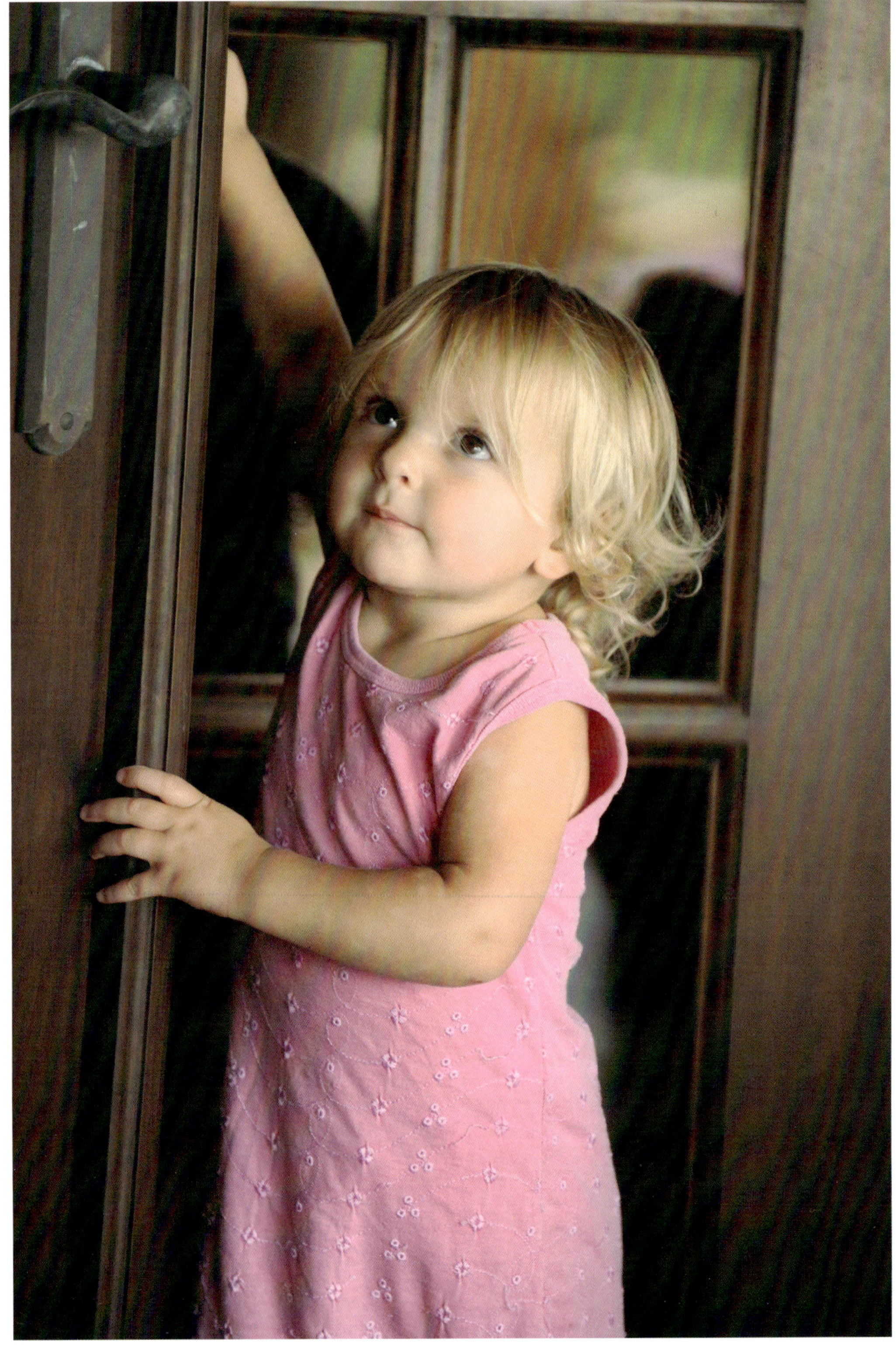

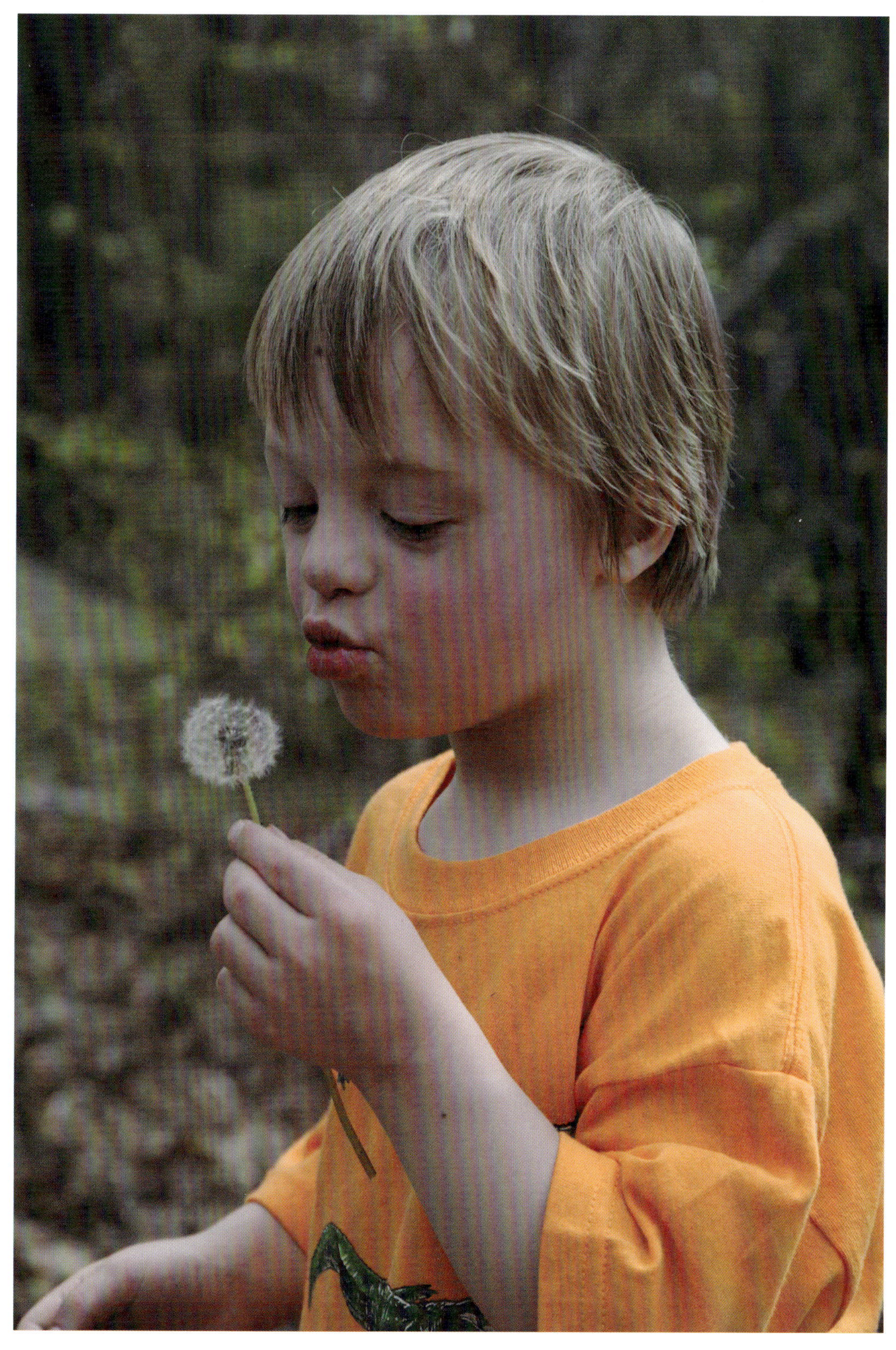

What if more older individuals or groups of seasoned citizens "adopted" struggling families and lent their time and energy to augment the emotional needs and supplement the time required to rear happy, healthy children?

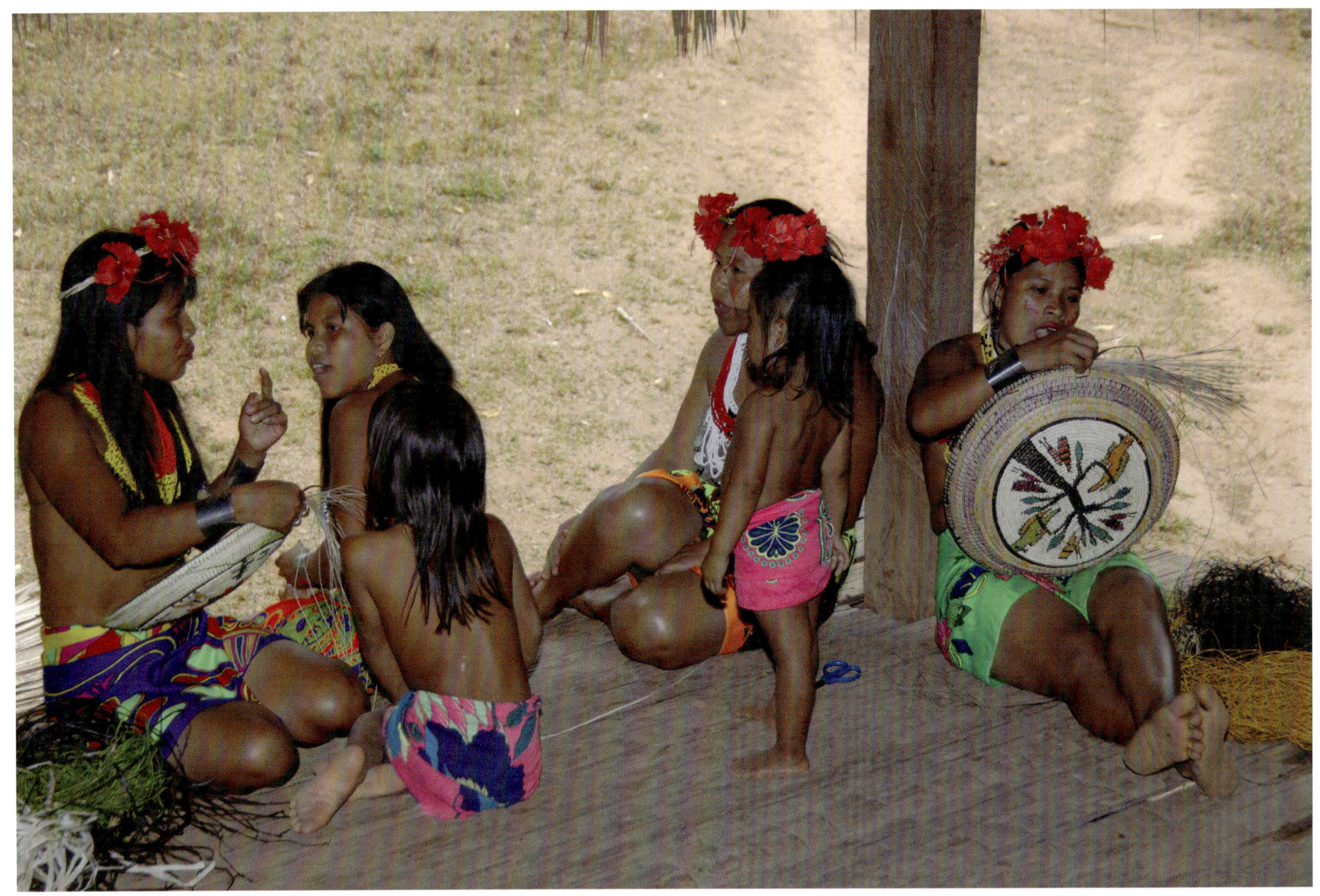

It does take a village. By deliberately engaging and adding continuity to the collective social fabric, perhaps the Baby Boomers will win back the respect previously accorded to older members of society in the early days of our nation's history.

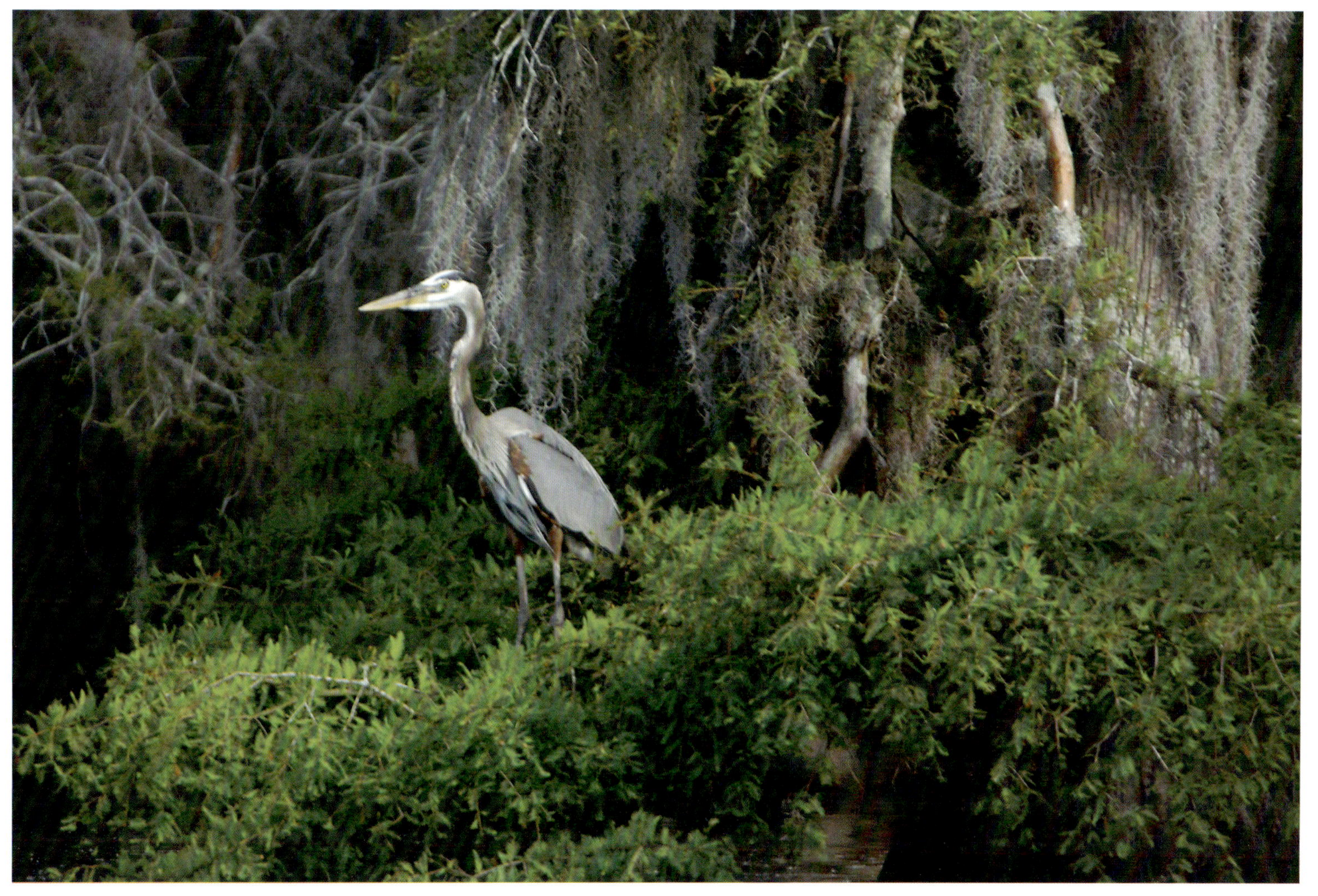

As poet and essayist Wendell Berry notes in his poem "There Is No Going Back," "Every day you have less reason not to give yourself away."

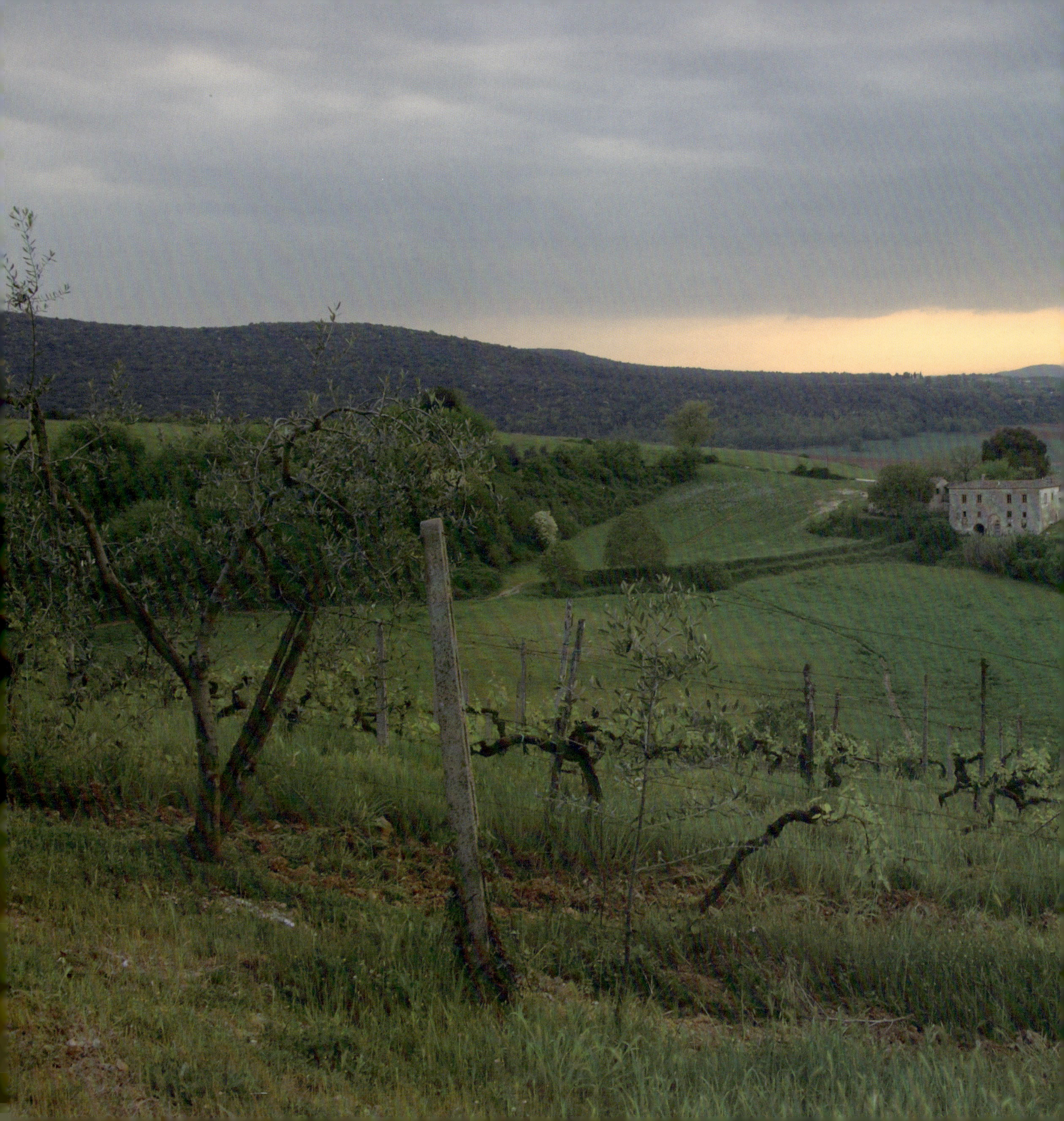

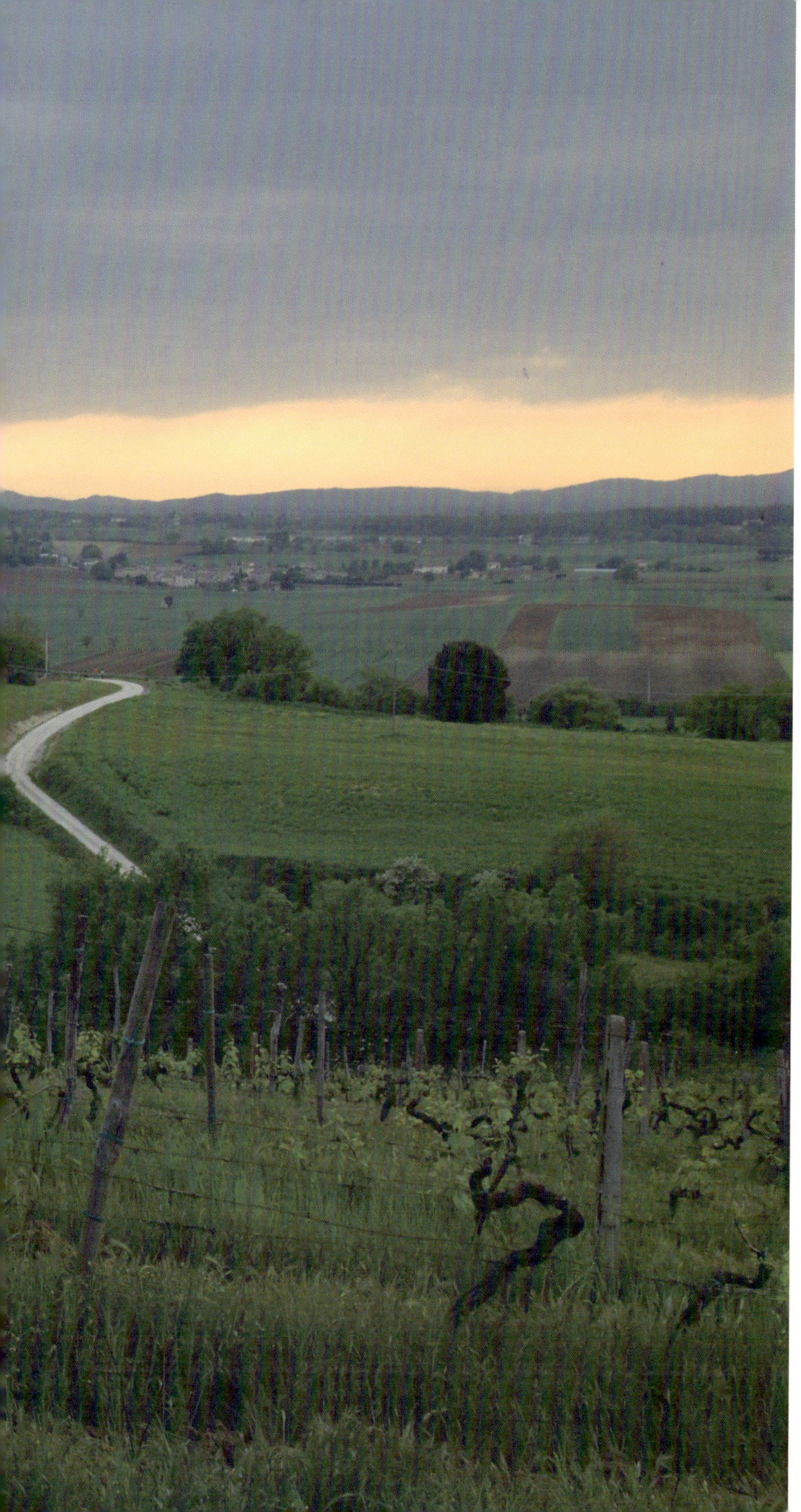

And so we've traveled through the seasons of the year and those of life. We have lovely memories of those earlier seasons, but we still have time to make more wonderful memories today, right now.

We still have time to picture our lives in a new way. If we choose to, we can open our eyes to the abundant beauty all around us, embrace a new perspective on aging, and savor the positives in every season we experience.

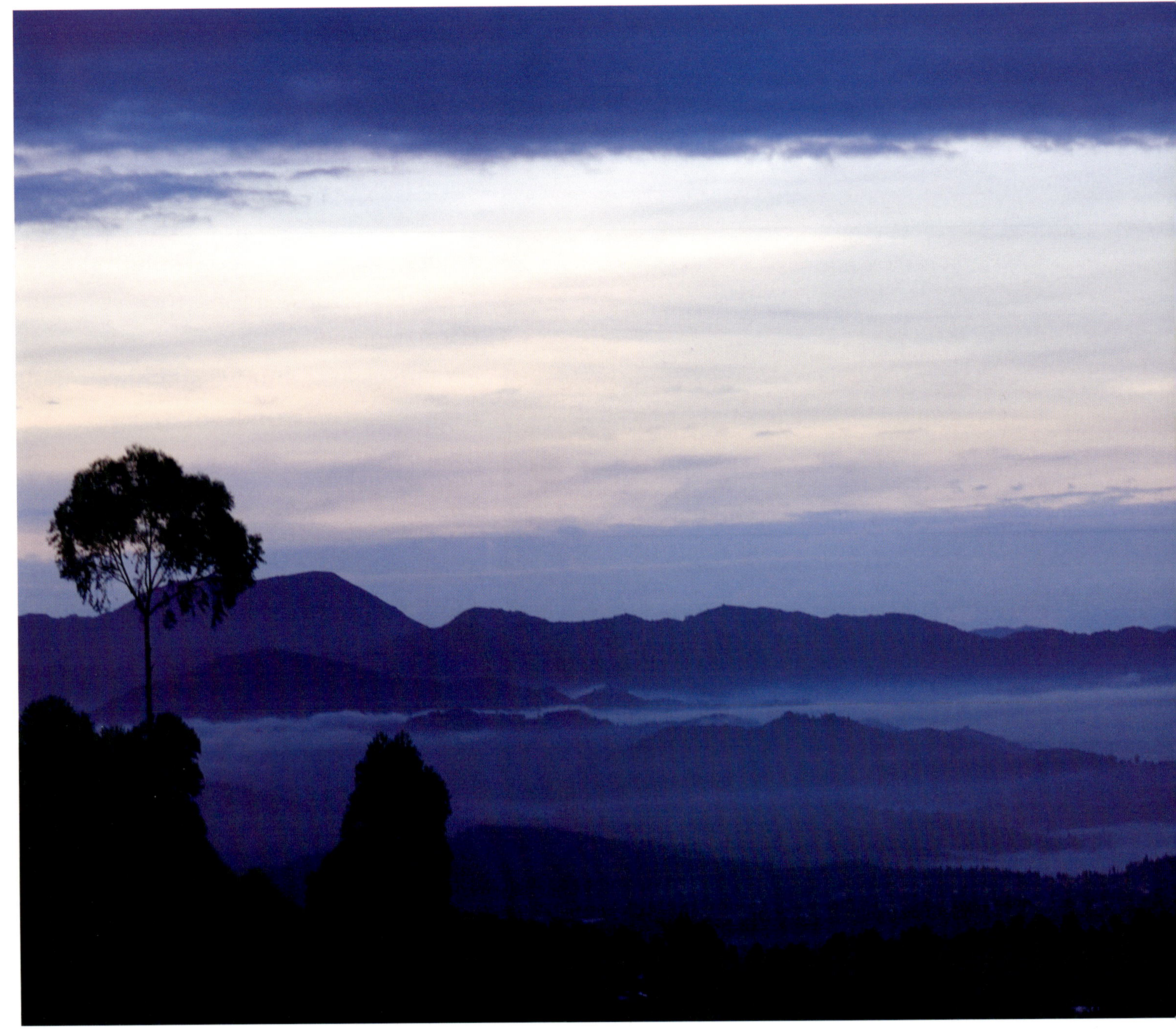

We no longer have overwhelming day-to-day responsibilities. Now is our time to try new things, to learn, to pick and choose where we give back, knowing that we want to live significant lives, to make the world better.

It's a new day. Spring is here. May we each make the most of it.

"Why stay we on the earth except to grow?"
Robert Browning, *Cleon*

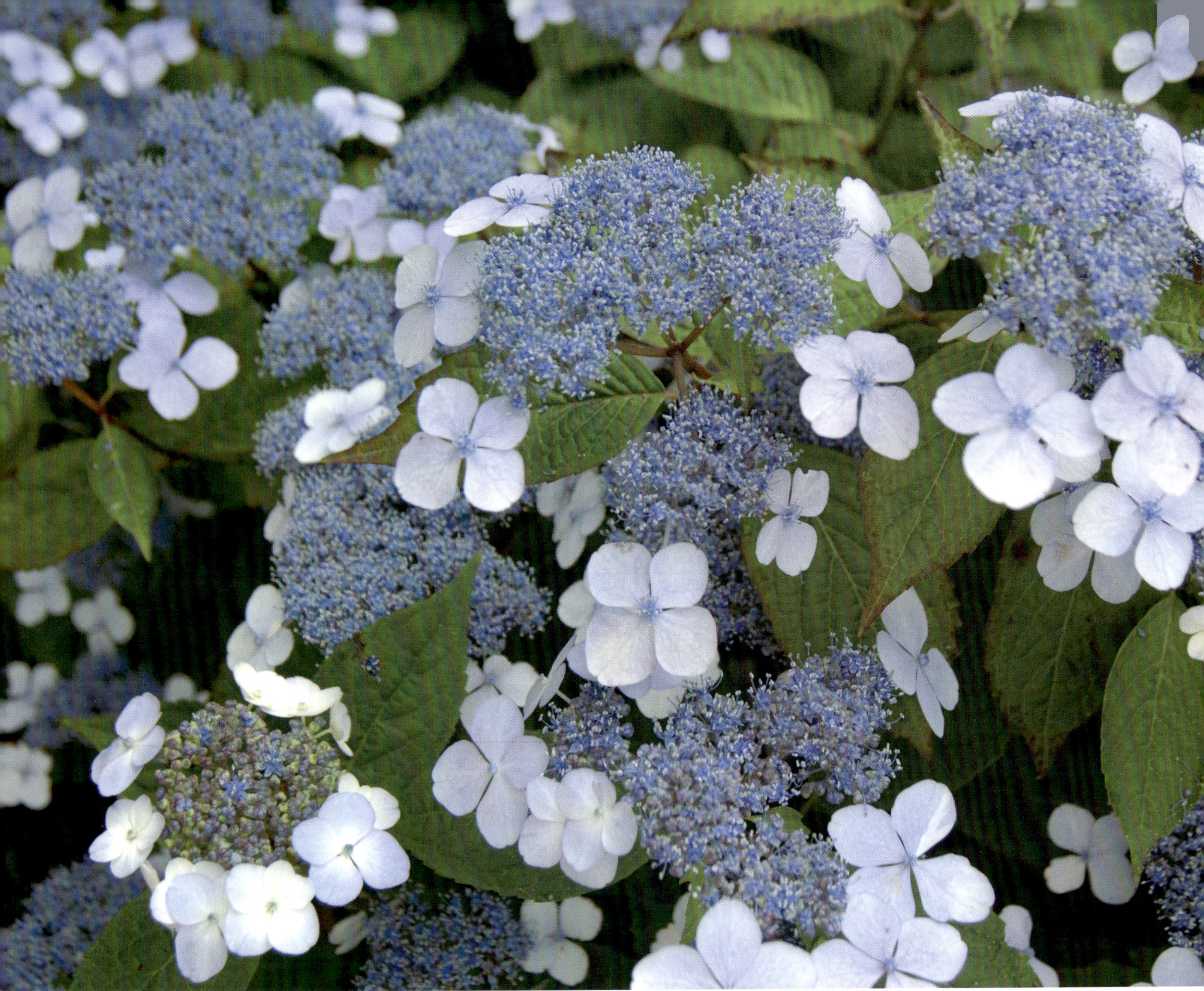

Lesson Learned in Spring

Cherish Each Day

Children seem to know from birth how to live in the moment. They are wound up when they get out of bed in the morning, and they move with enthusiasm from experience to experience, often devoting a mere ten minutes at a time to any given activity, all day long.

Remember how thrilling it was to experience all those firsts? Every day was an adventure. Our imaginations unfettered, we could go around the world – in our minds, at least – as pirates, cowboys, astronauts, or anything we chose.

The gift of wringing the most from each day seems to trickle away from us as we take on serious studies and responsibilities. Meanwhile, we use every waking moment to achieve specific goals that we think will make us smarter or richer or more popular. As these overriding goals permeate work or duty, our joy ebbs.

As youths, few of us have any expectation of dying any time soon, but we have no guarantees that we will live beyond the day we began this very morning.

Hold on to the excitement of the possibilities of a new day and savor its simple pleasures. This is one of the best recipes for well-being that exists. Recall the famous definition that states, "Happiness is being content with what you have."

Let us recognize the blessings of whatever and whomever we have and be grateful for this day, today. This will be one of the best long-term lessons – indeed, gifts – we'll ever learn.

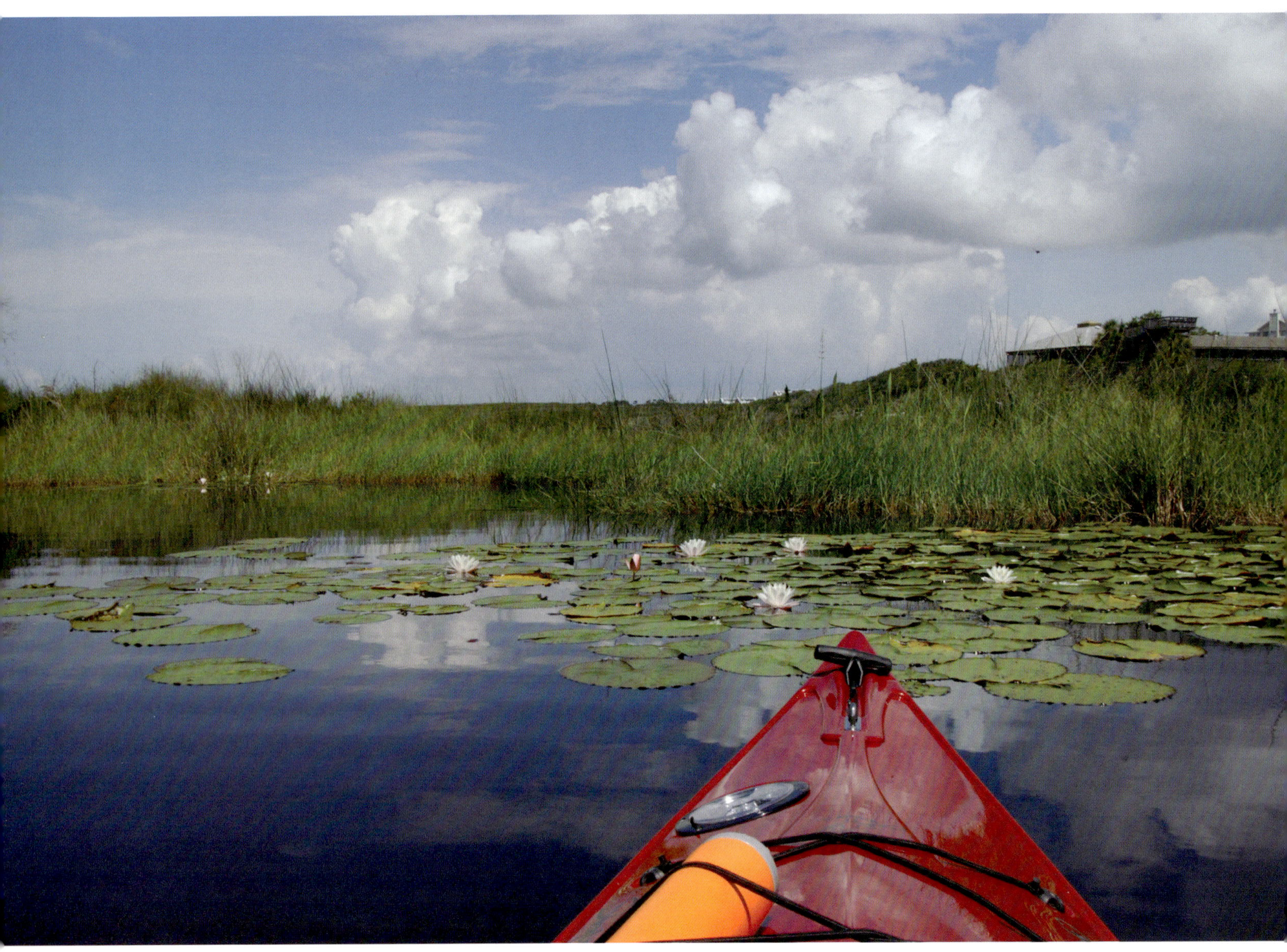

Your Thoughts on Your Seasons

Summer

1. What are some of your earliest memories from your first twenty years?

2. What person influenced you the most?

3. What did you fear the most in your first season?

4. How did you cope with that fear?

5. How would you characterize your religious or spiritual life?

6. Who was your best friend?

7. What lessons do you feel you learned about life during those first two decades?

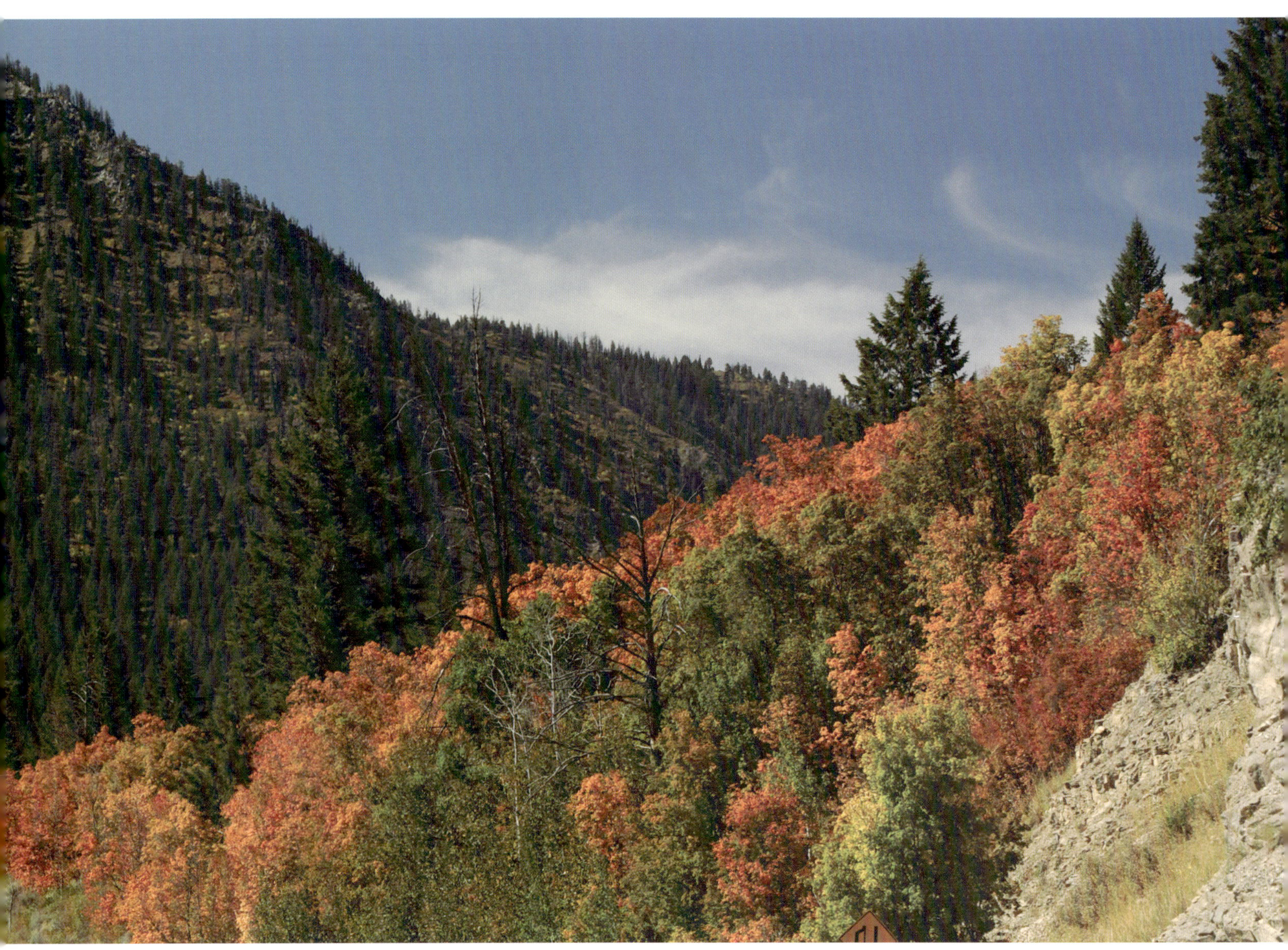

Your Thoughts on Your Seasons

Autumn

1. What person or people did you learn the most from during these two decades from ages twenty-one to forty?

2. Did you continue your formal education during that period? In retrospect, how valuable to you was this experience?

3. What was the hardest lesson you learned in your autumn?

4. What was one of your greatest joys? Was it unexpected?

5. Did you change careers or significant others during this time, and what lesson(s) did you learn?

6. What positives did you find yourself holding onto in this season of your life?

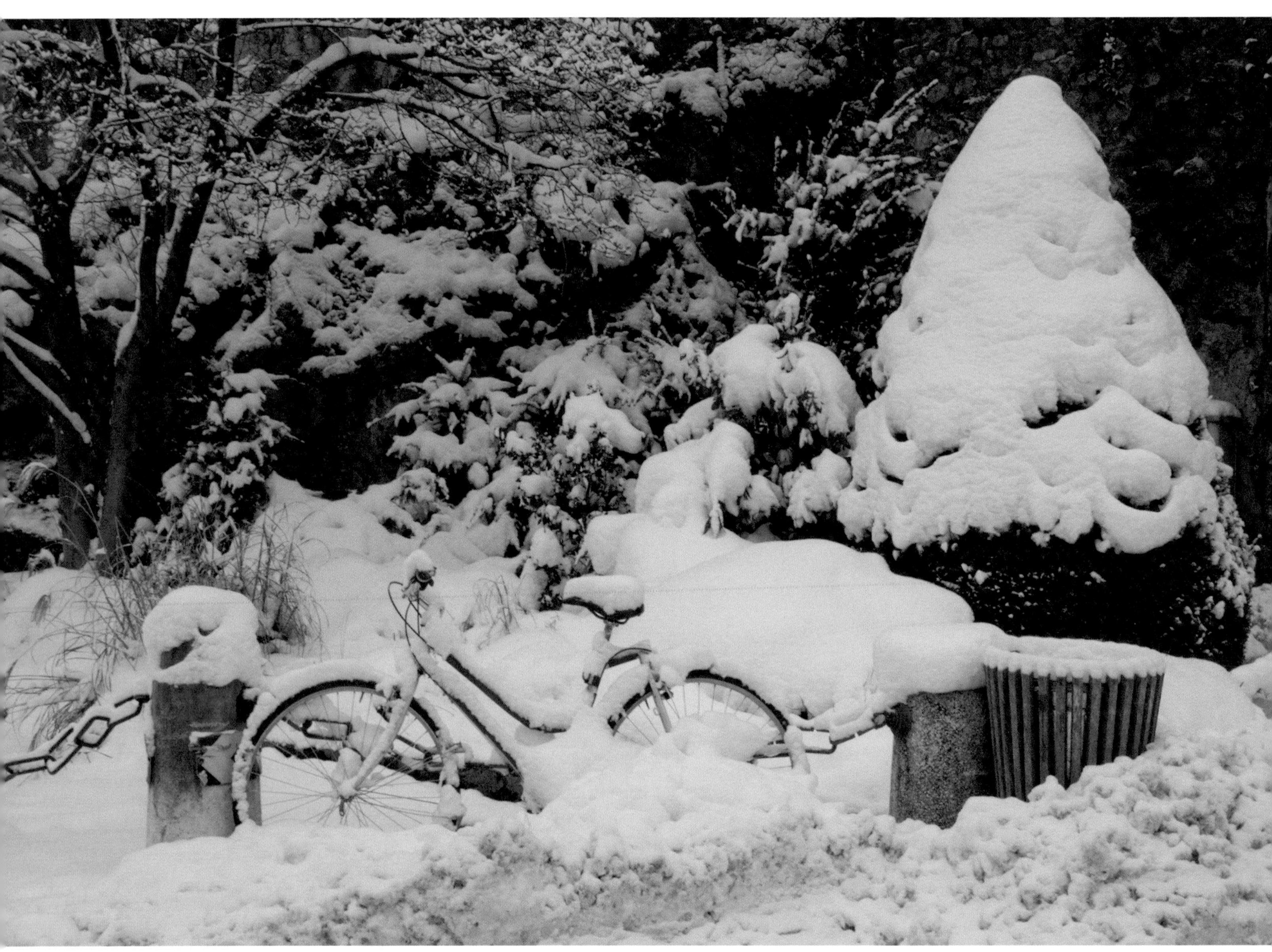

Your Thoughts on Your Seasons
Winter

1. How would you characterize, in a few words, this season of your life?

2. In what ways do you feel you have changed since the summer of your life?

3. Are you still in contact with any friends you had in your summer? If not, would you want to be? If so, why not reach out to them?

4. Do you have any strong relationships with people of other cultures?

5. Have you ever made an effort to go to a house of worship that is not of your faith?

6. What advice about living well might you give someone who is twenty-five years old?

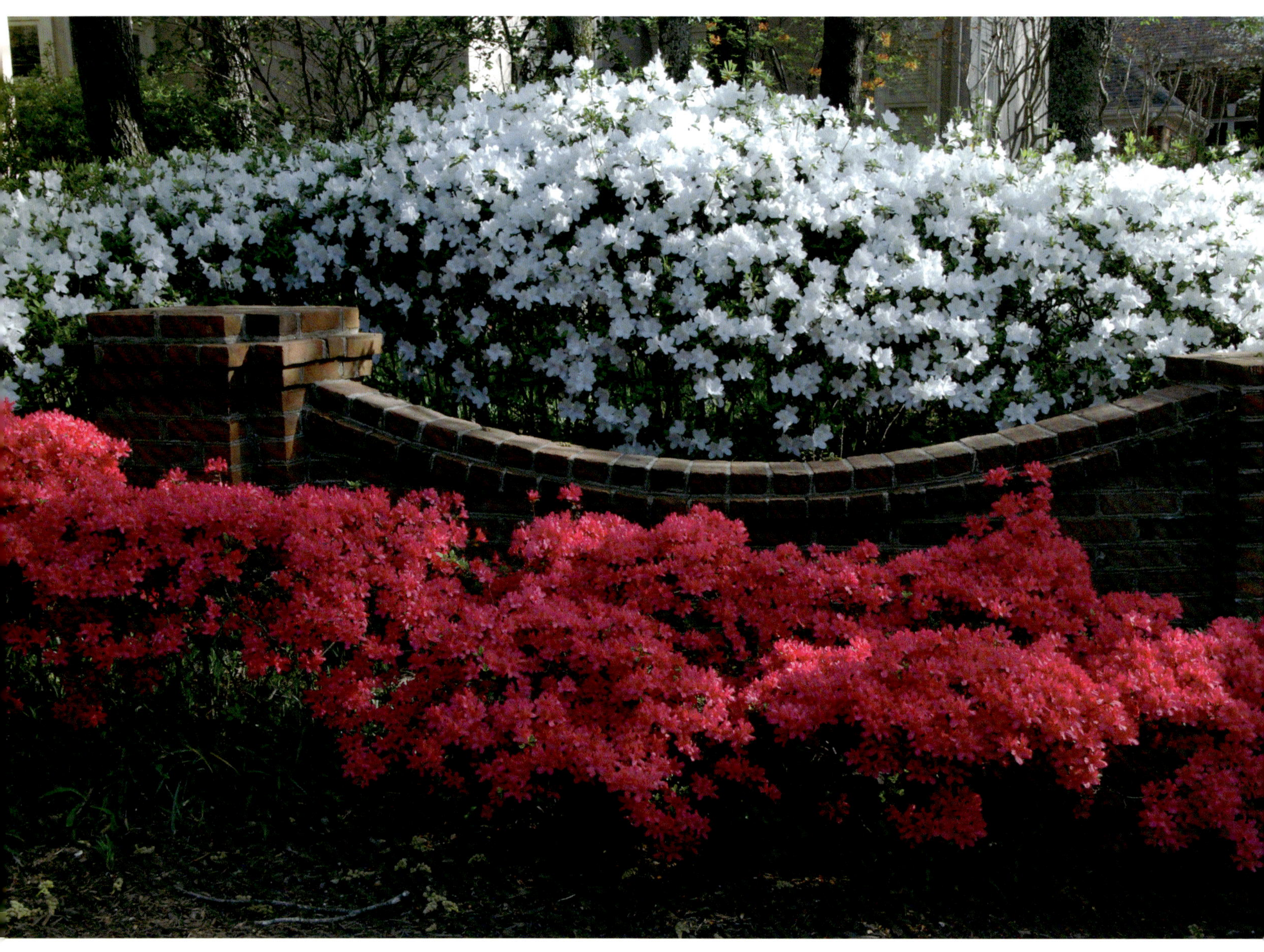

Your Thoughts on Your Seasons

Spring

1. As you reflect on earlier seasons, in which did you grow the most?

2. Which season was the most difficult to get through?

3. What helped you cope through that tough period?

4. How do you characterize this season you are in now?

5. What do you want to learn or do that you've not done, or done enough of, in the past?

6. What do you want friends or family to remember most about you?

7. What are you hopeful about in this season of your life?

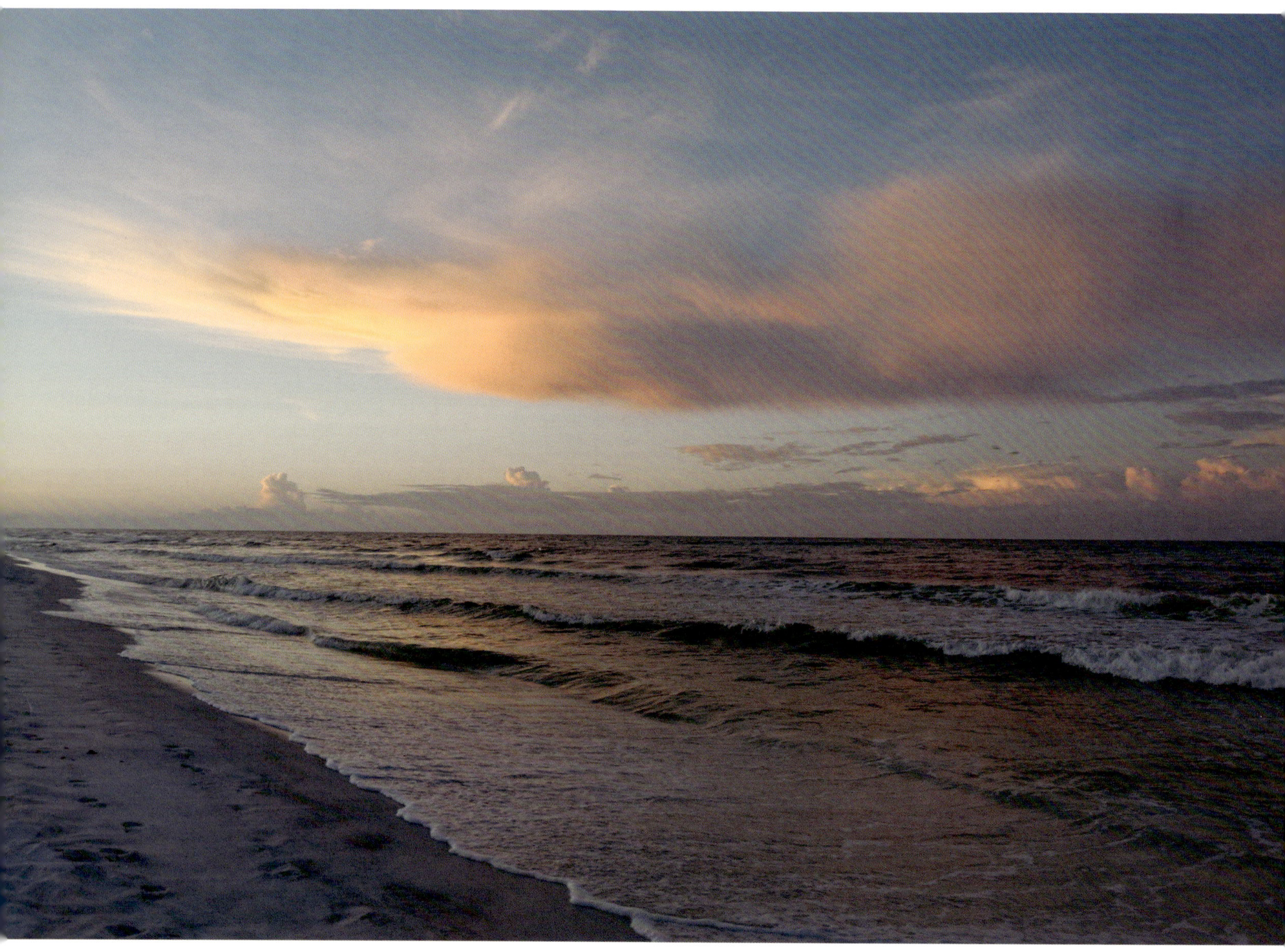

Author's Biography

Rebecca Webb Wilson

Rebecca Webb Wilson is an avid traveler and professional nature photographer (visit www.hawkeyenature.com) who has climbed Mt. Kilimanjaro, the Swiss Alps part of the Haute Route, and the Inca Trail to Machu Picchu. She began her love affair with travel when, upon college graduation, she became a stewardess with Pan American World Airways and flew all over the world.

After a brief stint as a realtor, Rebecca attended law school at the University of Memphis and served several years as an Assistant United States Attorney. Following that career and after the birth of her fourth child, she became involved with the Memphis Zoological Society in its efforts to remodel and revitalize its facility. In 1988, she founded a youth leadership program in Memphis called Bridge Builders, which to date has had 21,000 participants from all public, private, and parochial schools in Shelby County.

A graduate of Vanderbilt University, she serves as a member of its Board of Trust. Rebecca also serves on the board of directors of Baptist Memorial Health Care Corporation, which owns and operates fourteen hospitals in Tennessee, Arkansas, and Mississippi. One of *Memphis Woman Magazine*'s 50 Women Who Make a Difference, she received the Legends Award from the Women's Foundation for a Greater Memphis in 2010.

A deacon at Second Baptist Church in Memphis, Rebecca has authored meditations for adults and Sunday School materials for youth for Smyth and Helwys Publishers. She and her husband, Spence Lee Wilson, have two sons, two daughters, and nine grandchildren.

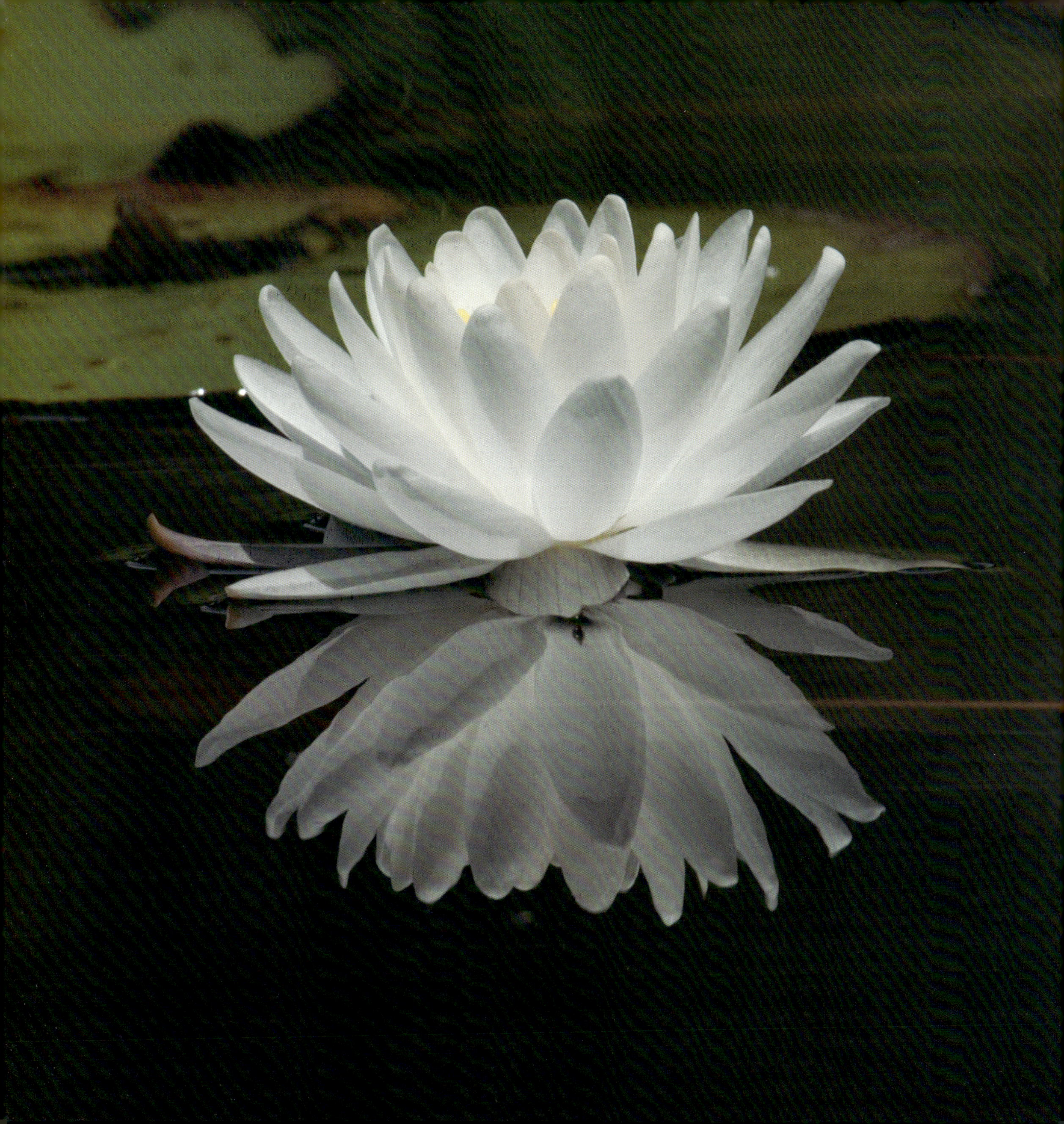